The Occult Trap

The Occult Trap

James S. Wallace

WAGNER
PUBLICATIONS

The Occult Trap
Copyright © 2004 by James S. Wallace
ISBN 1-58502-040-0

Published by
Wagner Publications
11005 N. Highway 83
Colorado Springs, CO 80921
www.wagnerpublications.org

Cover design by
eklektos
www.eklektosdesign.com

Edit and interior design by
Rebecca Sytsema

1 2 3 4 5 6 7 8 9   10 09 08 07 06 05 04

Table of Contents

Part One
SATAN AND DEMONS: A REAL ENEMY

Part Two
OCCULTISM: SATAN'S TRAP EXPOSED

Part Three
ESCAPING THE OCCULT TRAP: FREE AT LAST

Appendices

Table of Charts

Foreword

Way back in the 1980s when Peter and I began to become
involved in spiritual warfare, power ministries, intercession,
and deliverance, we had to formulate vocabulary for what God was
leading us to do and teach.

"The Third Wave of the Holy Spirit" was on the minds and
tongues of our circle of friends and colleagues. We began to pray
for the sick and see people healed! We began to pray fervently for
groups of people who had not yet heard the gospel and saw how
"power encounters" proved our God to be real and powerful—the
healer, the savior, the provider, the giver of peace, and so on. Prayer
for the sick and power encounters were new and powerful tools
added to the arsenal of equipment of many Christian workers.

But we weren't praying for the sick very long, nor were we
evangelizing out on the front lines much before we discovered the
reality of demons, principalities, and powers. We had to find out

how to deal with these dark angels. It was agreed upon that we were waging war out there on three different levels, which we called "ground-level," "occult-level," and "strategic-(or cosmic) level."

We defined "ground-level" as the casting out of demons from individuals. This was also called "deliverance." We see this again and again in Scripture. But over the course of the centuries, it seemed that the evangelical wing of the Church of Jesus Christ had lost the art of how to recognize when it was needed, and how to actually do it. At least it was totally absent from any pre-service training available to Peter and me before we headed for the mission field in the 1950s. We landed in enemy territory without the full inventory of equipment needed for spiritual warfare. Interestingly enough, because of our naiveté, we just didn't see demons, hence there was no need for the tools. Just as an aside, Peter and I saved up for a trip back to the places where we had served for 16 years in Bolivia. We made that trip to celebrate our 40th wedding anniversary, back in 1990. We were appalled by what we saw. All we could think of was "How could we have been so blind as not to have seen this?"

However, we could do much better now; so our passion is to better equip the body of Christ to work boldly in deliverance ministry and spiritual warfare. After all, Jesus did tell His disciples: "These signs will follow those who believe: In My name they will cast out demons; they will speak with new tongues, they will take up serpents, and if they drink anything deadly, it will by no means hurt them; they will lay hands on the sick and they will recover." It goes on to say, "And they went out and preached everywhere, the Lord working with them and confirming the word through the accompanying signs" (Mark 16:17-19, NKJV).

To me the interesting phrase in that passage of Scripture is "those who believe." There does not appear to be a time limit on those words, so I choose to believe that the description of Christians back then should also apply today. We have seen literally thousands of people healed and delivered. Victory breeds encouragement and enthusiasm.

Our group of colleagues then discerned that there were two other levels of demonic activity that seemed to be more organized and powerful. "Occult-level" warfare dealt with the demonic activity occurring in things like Satanism, witchcraft, shamanism, curanderos, Freemasonry, and the like. Worship of certain demonic beings seemed to be included with this level. It would take a little more understanding to deal with those who had been deeply involved with these systems. Often a very deep level of inner healing is required to bring people into total freedom. But freedom is possible. Some of the finest Christian workers I know have come out of the occult, and today are totally fearless because they know how much more powerful Christ is than the demons that once held them captive.

Then, of course, strategic-level spiritual warfare deals with powerful principalities and powers that hold territories, people groups, and systems under their sway. Those who combat these powerful spirits are specialists who are few in number and like our "special forces" in the military. Not many are needed, actually. They pray prophetic prayers and do battle in the heavenlies accompanied by prophetic acts and spiritual warfare.

These warriors are in touch with God on a special level and we don't talk a whole lot about this because, frankly, most Christians do not understand it—nor do they need to. Special forces are rather private in nature. But if the other foot soldiers ("those who believe") keep busy with what they are supposed to do (casting out demons) the governmental structure of evil will continue to be weakened and more and more souls will be snatched from its kingdom of darkness into the kingdom of light.

Literature in the field of ground-level spiritual warfare (casting out demons) is plentiful, if you know where to look for it. Our ministry, Global Harvest Ministries, started a bookstore called "The Arsenal" with the view of bringing together many resources from wherever we could find them, so as to help the body of Christ become better equipped for battle. For those interested, these resources can be found at www.arsenalbooks.com.

But, we were always shy on books having to do with the occult-level warfare. There are some, but we needed a basic text in the field that we could recommend. And now the book you hold in your hands is a very good start. I was delighted to get the manuscript from Jim Wallace. I immediately liked it because it was written in an organized, scholarly (but not ponderous) manner. I felt a kindred spirit with Jim because he came from much the same theological tradition Peter and I did, and he learned much of what he knows from practical experience on the mission field. We sort of wound our way through the same pilgrimage and came out at the same place. Of course, my prophet friends would say something like: "Well, what would you expect—it's what the Spirit is saying to the churches."

I wish every deliverance minister out there could get a copy of this book. Pastors, youth ministers, and parents would greatly benefit from reading this also. Fear is a weapon of warfare *from the enemy*. It is often the only thing that keeps God's people from coming against the demonic, especially the occult level. Actually, friends, the demons fear equipped Christians a whole lot more than we can possibly fear them because we have the power to undo them.

Understanding the strategy of the enemy and his modus operandi is the first step in defeating him. The intelligence contained in this book can deal an enormous blow to the kingdom of darkness if put to use.

The clear step-by-step examples to assist both deliverance ministers, and even those who can't find help from a qualified deliverance minister, are excellent! Thanks, Jim, for placing in order this rather unsavory topic so as to better equip the body of Christ for war.

Saints, let's get with the program and put this valuable material to use. We can be an integral part of the prayer Jesus taught us to pray: "Thy Kingdom come."

Doris M. Wagner
Global Harvest Ministries
International Society of Deliverance Ministers
Colorado Springs, Colorado

Acknowledgments

I would like to acknowledge and thank a number of people who have had a significant impact on my life and ministry over the years. Each, in their own way, has taught me much about the love and grace of God and His power to set us free to live life fully.

Rev. Percy Burns, a wonderful pastor and mentor, who early in my Christian life took me under his wing to disciple and equip for ministry, showing me the reality and practicality of "power" ministry.

The church planting and ministry team we worked with in the Philippines—Eilish Agnew, Alan and Edna Ashton, Mary Bates, Mike Baldemoro, Lem Demadura, Karen Lampinen, Michael and Dawn Rablen, and Nora Rimmer. Not only were they wonderful friends, but together we discussed and analyzed different approaches to doing ministry and, through trial and error, learned much about the practical outworking of ministry.

Cornerstone Bible Christian Fellowship in Quezon City, Philippines. This was our church family, an exceptional group of people who love the Lord wholeheartedly and follow Him faithfully. The knowledge and insights gained from them have been invaluable.

Mark and Lois Stephenson, faithful friends who have stood beside us through many trials and gave me special encouragement to pursue this book project.

Rev. Jim and Linda Hatcher, lifelong friends who are just that, true friends with whom you can share life heart to heart. Jim has since gone to be with the Lord, but his impact and influence live on.

Doris Wagner, a new friend whom I highly respect, received this manuscript warmly and enthusiastically from a very unsure first-time writer. She gave me wise counsel and advice and walked me through the process of publishing, along with the wonderful staff at Wagner Publications.

My daughters, Christy, Erin, Jenny, and Stephanie, each of whom is a real beauty. At times, as all kids do, they have put me to the test, but unquestionably they are my joy and delight. How wonderful to know that they are each faithfully following the Lord. My oldest daughter, Christy, has in particular taken an interest in this project and has repeatedly encouraged me not to give up.

And finally, I would like to recognize my wife of twenty-six years, Penny. She is an incredible woman of great fortitude and perseverance, a deeply insightful and powerful intercessor, and a loyal and faithful partner and friend, not to mention a wonderful mother. What a gift of God she has been to me, walking side by side through the ups and downs of life, doing ministry together, and being a sounding board for ideas. Without a doubt, the achievements in my life, including this book, would have been impossible without her.

For all these people, and for the goodness of God has shown to me in Christ, I am eternally grateful. Truly, I am a wealthy man, greatly blessed.

Introduction

*W*e live in a day and age when we have been educated to believe that everything can be explained in natural or scientific terms. We tend to think that human intelligence, reason, and technological advances can solve every problem. However, in spite of this teaching, we see in our experience and that of others, this is not the case. Science and reason just don't seem to be able to adequately explain *all* the events we see happening in the world around us or that we have experienced personally.

Many people are looking for alternative explanations. And so we observe a resurgence of interest in religion and in occultism. Both of these deal with an acknowledgment of supernatural forces or powers which are above and beyond the realm of the natural world. They are forces that cannot be investigated or known strictly on the basis of empirical scientific research, or resolved by logic.

Yet turning to religion and spirituality does not always lead to the truth and a full, enjoyable relationship with God. Based upon the special revelation of holy Scripture, we know that apart from the one true and living God, there are many demonic beings posing as gods, striving under the leadership of Satan to lead men and women astray from the truth. And the world's religions are filled with the worship and veneration of innumerable false deities and demigods.

The fact is, most of the people living in the world today, even the spiritual ones, are living in darkness and deception, with their spiritual eyes blinded to a true knowledge of God and spiritual realities (see 2 Cor. 4:4). These people are destined, to a lesser or greater degree, to live in spiritual bondage under Satan's dominion unless and until they are personally set free through an encounter with the Lord Jesus Christ.

One of the dominant aspects of non-Christian religions, whether they be highly systematized and developed belief systems, or very simple, is that virtually all incorporate some elements of the occult. Divination, magic, and spiritism permeate the religious and spiritual life of every culture and people group in the world; some more evident than others, but present in all nonetheless. Even unaware Christians may be taken in by the deceptive lure of the occult. And so, many people through their participation with occult practices have come under a particularly intense form of spiritual bondage to Satan. In some cases, this may result in some form of actual demonization. Thus, the effect of the occult on people's lives can be devastating.

In the years I have spent in ministry, I have seen an alarming ignorance on the part of many Christians to the reality of Satan and demons and the spiritual conflict that is constantly taking place. Many take a very nonchalant attitude toward spiritual warfare, demonization, and occultism in its various forms. This lack of awareness and concern can have a harmful effect on their individual lives and on the overall health of the church – not to mention handicapping the church in one of the most vital areas of her ministry and outreach to the world.

It has been encouraging to see in recent years a number of fine books published which investigate various aspects of this spiritual conflict and explain how God has equipped His church to engage in the battle triumphantly (many of these have been consulted in the preparation of this work and are referenced in the footnotes). I have intended this book to be a practical handbook, drawing together some of the foundational material on spiritual warfare in a concise form and including an exposé on occultism.

It is my hope that it will serve to enlighten Christians and seekers of the truth by exposing the works of Satan through the occult in which they may have unknowingly been participating. With the intensification of the spiritual conflict in our day, Christians need to be enabled to discern the difference between the power of God and the power of Satan, so that they are not deceived, but effectively overcome the works of the enemy. It is also my desire that this will be an effective reference tool for pastors and church workers to aid them in ministering to those under their care.

With these objectives in mind, it is my purpose to present a biblical view of Satan and demons and their activity; to explain the occult in its three main areas—divination, magic, and spiritism—and list and define various common practices of each; to present a biblical view and analysis of the occult; to present a criteria by which Christians can evaluate alleged supernatural phenomena and discern the true source behind it, whether it be of God or Satan; and to present a method of deliverance that can be followed to free people from occult bondage.

It has been said that there are two approaches to discerning between good and evil. One is to know Satan and his works so well that when you see them you will easily recognize them. The other, is to get to know Jesus Christ well, so that if you see any deviation from His truth, you will recognize it.

Let me state emphatically from the outset, that the overriding focus and center of our lives must be the Lord Jesus Christ. This must ever be our highest goal in life—to know God and live in fellowship with Him. The better we know Him, the more intimate we are with Him, and the more sensitive we are to His Spirit, the easier is will be to discern between truth and error, between works of God and works of Satan. The closer we are to Him, the more clearly will we recognize those things that are out of harmony with Him. Nevertheless, it is important to know our enemy and this book seeks to expose the enemy and his works through the occult to the light of God's truth.

> " ... if the Son sets you free, you will be free indeed."
> —John 8:36, NIV

Part One

Satan and Demons:
A Real Enemy

Chapter One

Kingdoms in Conflict

As we begin our look into freedom from the occult trap, it is important to see the activity of Satan, demons, and occultism in the overall context of spiritual conflict. It is easy both to overestimate and underestimate the extent of the power and influence of Satan. Overestimating his power can generate an unnecessary sense of fear and create a feeling of inability to confront him successfully. Underestimating his power could carelessly open one to unnecessary risks and harm.

Yet, if we have an overall understanding of the spiritual conflict between the kingdom of God and the kingdom of Satan, we will be able to see that although we need to have a healthy respect for our adversary, we need not fear him. On the contrary, we will understand that he is overcome through Christ, and that in Christ, we can experience true liberty.

The Meaning of "Kingdom"

The Bible speaks to us of two kingdoms on the earth—The kingdom of God and the kingdom of Satan. What do we mean when we speak of "kingdom?" George Eldon Ladd explains what is meant when the Bible uses the phrase "kingdom of God."[1] He says that, "it always refers to His reign, His rule, His sovereignty, and not to the realm in which it is exercised."[2] So then, the term "kingdom" here, does not mean the territory or realm over which a king rules, but rather it speaks of a king's authority and the exercise of his rule over his subjects. Thus, these two kingdoms are not visible kingdoms, but spiritual. These two kingdoms are evidenced by their respective rule in people's lives. Those who are subject to Satan's rule are living in his kingdom, while those who are subject to God's rule are living in the kingdom of God.

The Kingdom of Satan

When Jesus was led out into the wilderness to be tempted, Satan led Him up to a high place and showed Him all the kingdoms of this world. Satan said that all these kingdoms had been given to him and that he would give them to Jesus if only Jesus would worship him (Lk. 4:5-8). Jesus did not dispute Satan's authority or rulership over the kingdoms of the world. He did not say that Satan did not have this power. But He simply refused to worship Satan, saying that all worship belonged to God alone.

The day would come, in God's time and in God's way, in which it would be fulfilled that, "The kingdom of this world has become

---

[1] The term "kingdom of God" may be used interchangeably with "kingdom of heaven." They both refer to the same thing.

[2] George E. Ladd, *The Gospel and the Kingdom* (Grand Rapids, MI: Eerdman's, 1959), p. 20.

the kingdom of our Lord and of his Christ and he will reign forever and ever" (Rev. 11:15). Satan has been given authority over the kingdoms of this world, though as we shall see, it is limited and temporary.

How did Satan obtain this authority? This tragic occurrence dates back to the first man and woman. When God created man and woman in the Garden of Eden, He gave them authority over the earth—to manage and care for it and all its creatures (Gen. 1:27-30). But when Satan, in the guise of a serpent, tempted Eve, she and Adam heeded his deceptive words rather than remain obedient to God (Gen. 3:1-7). Through the fall, humanity surrendered their dominion over the earth to Satan. Satan is now described as the "prince of this world" (Jn. 12:31) or "ruler of the kingdom of the air" (Eph. 2:2).

Satan has been in rebellion against God since before humanity appeared on the scene. Satan's kingdom has no more in common with the kingdom of God than oil has with water—the two don't mix. In his enmity toward God, Satan wants to stifle the life of the kingdom of God in men and women. He may do this directly through his own personal activity in their lives. He may for example, snatch away the seed of the word of God sown in individual hearts (Matt. 13:19). He might also work indirectly through the individuals, ideas, and events under his rule, which he manipulates to lead people away from God (Matt. 13:22).

Jesus and the Kingdom of God

From before time, God has had a plan to regain rightful rule over all the peoples of the earth. There were two outstanding purposes underlying all that Jesus said or did throughout His ministry and in His death and resurrection. Jesus came to evict Satan, ending his rule over humanity, and to restore God's kingdom.

The Father sent Jesus to destroy the works of the kingdom of Satan (Jn. 12:31; 1 Jn. 3:8). Jesus came in a sense as a divine invader to destroy demons and release men and women to eternal life; which explains why the Lord's presence caused demons to tremble and fear. His ministry was marked by a continual conflict with Satan and demons for the purpose of establishing God's reign on earth.[3] By His very presence, and by what He said and did, Jesus inaugurated the kingdom of God on earth.

Jesus carried out His public ministry not only by proclaiming the arrival of the kingdom of God, but also by demonstrating the power of this kingdom. He did this through healing the sick, raising the dead, and casting out demons. "That evening after sunset the people brought to Jesus all the sick and demon-possessed. The whole town gathered at the door, and Jesus healed many who had various diseases. He also drove out many demons..." (Mk. 1:32-34). In these mighty acts, Jesus demonstrated His power and authority.

In the casting out of demons Jesus showed His superiority over Satan and his demon cohorts and announced the downfall of Satan's kingdom. He showed that true power and authority belong to God alone. In one instance, Jesus delivered a man from demonic bondage that had caused him to be blind and mute. Some controversy arose about the source of Jesus' authority to do this, even to the point of accusing Him of casting out demons by the prince of demons. Jesus replied that it was not by the prince of demons, for Satan would not drive out Satan. But rather, "if I drive out demons

---

[3] For example, Herod's plan against the baby Jesus; Jesus' temptation in the wilderness; Jesus' casting out demons; attempts on Jesus' life before the proper time; Peter's argument with Jesus to dissuade Him from the cross; and the cross itself.

by the Spirit of God, then the kingdom of God has come upon you" (Matt. 12:28).

Here, Jesus clearly says that His power to cast out evil spirits heralds the arrival of a greater and stronger kingdom than that of Satan—the kingdom of God. The previously unquestioned power and authority of Satan have now been broken by Jesus Christ. Furthermore, as Ladd writes, "...men and women are delivered from the power of Satan that they may enter into the power and the life and the blessing of the Kingdom of God."[4]

The Nature of the Conflict

The kingdom of God has indeed come into the world. It is a source of daily strength for those who live in it and it is the source of salvation for those who respond to its call for conversion. By His death and resurrection, the Lord Jesus Christ has overthrown the kingdom of Satan. At the same time, we are confronted with the fact that we do not yet enjoy the fullness of the kingdom of God. For that, we await the consummation of God's plan at the return of the Lord. In the meantime, we find ourselves in the midst of a spiritual battle—not as observers, but as participants.

In coming into a relationship with Christ, we receive eternal life, forgiveness of sins, and a new nature. We are released from bondage to the kingdom of Satan and given life in the kingdom of God. As we walk with God, we have access to His protection from Satan's harm and are enabled to overcome Satan (1 Jn. 5:18). However, Satan is still active and as John tells us, "the whole world is under the control of the evil one" (1 Jn. 5:19). Those who have not yet turned to Christ are Satan's prey, and he also continues to war

---

[4] Ladd, p.50.

on Christian believers. So, although we have all that we need for eternal life, nevertheless, we live in a hostile environment, dominated by Satan. His ultimate power and claim have been broken through Christ, but sin, sickness, and death continue to afflict us. Satan knows his ultimate defeat has already been assured, but he continues his struggle, destroying as much as he can before his power is forever taken from him.

Our Role in the Conflict

The followers of the Lord Jesus were given a task—to make disciples of all nations and to extend God's kingdom to the ends of the earth. The message of the Kingdom which He proclaimed, He passed on to His disciples. This message acknowledges the helpless condition of humanity—that people have fallen from the relationship they once enjoyed with God and are incapable on their own of regaining it; that they have placed themselves in bondage to sin and are a slave to it; and that they are under the dominion of the "ruler of this world."

To a sinful human race, the message of the kingdom of God proclaims the only effective remedy—salvation has come through faith in Jesus Christ, the Son of God; Christ has won the victory over death, He has defeated Satan, and the power of sin has been broken. For those who receive this message the Scripture declares, "he has rescued us from the dominion of darkness and brought us into the kingdom of the Son he loves, in whom we have redemption, the forgiveness of sins" (Col. 1:13-14).

The task of proclaiming the Kingdom cannot be fulfilled through words alone. It must be accomplished also through a clear demonstration of the Kingdom's power and presence. When people experience the works of God in their lives in tangible ways, the words of the gospel become alive with meaning. Dr. J. Rodman

Williams has observed that there is a "vital connection between proclamation of the gospel and the attestation of miracles in declaring the living reality of Christ and in bringing about faith and obedience."[5] The works that Jesus did in announcing the kingdom of God and demonstrating that it had in fact already come, must also be performed by Jesus' followers today (Jn. 14:12). The same demonstrations of power which Jesus used in His ministry to tear down Satan's strongholds, He has granted to us to further His kingdom here and now. They are available until that day when He returns and ushers in the Kingdom in all its fullness.

We live in the interim period between the mortal death blow dealt to Satan on the cross and the final destruction of his kingdom when the Lord comes again. The fact of Satan's open warfare on Christian believers, combined with Christ's command that we "make disciples of all nations" (Matt. 28:18-19), means we are locked into spiritual warfare until Christ's return. We are called to liberate captives for Jesus Christ, to take back for the kingdom of God that which has been dominated by Satan. As we advance in this warfare, the victims of Satan's power are released, and the time for the ending of Satan's dominion and the establishment of God's rule comes nearer.

As followers of the Lord Jesus Christ and subjects of His kingdom, we must face the enemy and fight him with the equipping and strength that the Lord provides. Like Jesus Himself, we have a job to do. Our job is to proclaim the kingdom of God to all peoples and demonstrate it through signs and wonders—healing the sick and casting out demons (Mk. 16:15-18). Just as Jesus was sent on a mission from the Father, so has He now sent us on a mission (Jn.

[5] Williams, J. Rodman, *Renewal Theology: God, the World, & Redemption*, Vol. 1 (Grand Rapids, MI: Zondervan, 1988), p. 153.

20:21). The works that He did, are the works that we too should do (Jn. 12:14).

Scripture is clear about the seriousness and centrality of spiritual warfare for the believer. Peter warns us to be on the alert, for Satan is like a lion on the prowl, seeking someone to devour (1 Pet. 5:8-9). Paul also explains that we battle against unseen spiritual forces of evil and that we must therefore be clothed in the armor of God (Eph. 6:10-12). Spiritual warfare is a fact in the conflict between the kingdom of God and the kingdom of Satan. It is unavoidable. But this should not frighten us, for what every Christian needs to know about spiritual warfare is that while Satan is strong, Christ is stronger. We have nothing to fear from Satan or demons, as long as we live faithfully and righteously in Christ, walking by the power of the Spirit, and never backing down when challenged by evil.

Summary

And so, there are two kingdoms—God's and Satan's—which presently exist side by side. Satan's kingdom is in rebellion against God's rule and hostile to the gospel. This world and the age we're living in are dominated by evil and under Satan's dominion. He rules over the lives of every person who is not living in right relationship with God through Jesus Christ.

At the same time, God's reign (Kingdom) has come into the world in the person of Jesus Christ (Matt. 12:28) and we may experience something of its power and its blessings now. By repenting of personal sin and believing in Jesus Christ, men and women are redeemed from the world, the flesh, and the devil, and they come under the reign of God's Kingdom (Jn. 3:1-21). So then, the Kingdom is made up of all those who have come to the Lord and have been brought out of bondage to the kingdom of darkness. Those who are in God's Kingdom have been freed from enslavement and no longer have to live in conformity with this world.

Yet there is still a spiritual conflict taking place. While Satan does have authority over the earth, that authority is limited. The kingdom of God is destroying the kingdom of Satan (1 Jn. 3:8). The outcome of the conflict has been assured through the cross of Jesus Christ (Col. 2:15). Although God's Kingdom is not yet here in its fullness, it will be fully established, and the kingdom of Satan will be eternally destroyed at the return of the Lord Jesus Christ (Matt. 13:36-43).

Chapter Two

Satan and Demons

*T*o win a war, a game, or a contest, there are three things which are vital to know. First, you must recognize that there is an opponent. This seems very obvious, yet when it comes to the area of spiritual warfare, many people are not aware that they have an enemy who is out to destroy them. This chapter will identify who that enemy is. Second, it is helpful to know your enemy or opponent well; that is, you should know something about what he does (his work), and how he does it (his methods). In this way you can prepare a defense against his attacks as well as prepare an appropriate offense to overcome him. Third, you need to know how to carry on the battle against him. These are the things this chapter will set forth.

Are Satan and Demons for Real?

There are many people who find it difficult to believe in the existence of Satan and demons. Some feel that with the "age of enlightenment" and our advances in technology and psychology, everything can be explained purely in scientific terms. To them, Satan and demons, and the phenomena associated with them, are explained away as nothing more than myths, folk tales, and superstition. For others, the thought of evil beings opposing human beings frightens them and so they choose to ignore them, hoping they will go away. Neither of these approaches however, adequately confronts the question of Satan's existence.

The Testimony of Human History and Experience

When the wind blows through the trees, we don't see the wind, but we do see the evidence of its passing. Likewise, looking at the record of human history and experience we may not see Satan, but we can see ample evidence of his presence and activity. The daily news is highlighted by reports of crime, often degrading—inhuman crimes of violence, sometimes so bizarre as to virtually defy comprehension. Crimes which are committed without conscience or remorse. We don't have to look too far to see a multiplicity of moral sins in many perverse variations—adultery, child pornography and pedophilia, bisexuality, homosexuality, transvestitism, and sadomasochism. There has also been the explosion of heresies, cults, and false religions—seducing spirits propagating the doctrines of demons.

In the 20th century, which was to have shown the highest of human social, moral, and technological achievements and advances, there occurred some of the greatest atrocities humanity has ever known: the Nazi atrocities and Jewish holocaust of World War II; Stalin's purges in Russia; the genocide in Cambodia in 1975-78 (during which time Pol Pot and the Khmer Rouge exterminated nearly one-third of the total population of 2.3 million people); not to mention vicious tribal warfare and genocide in Africa. Even the ethnic strife that has been witnessed more recently in the nations under the former Soviet umbrella has demonstrated great brutality and cruelty. And of course, there are the many murderous acts of terrorism that now plague every corner of the globe. The depth of evil being expressed in much of this behavior is so great that it is not sufficient to explain the inspiration of these events merely in terms of mental illness or even human sinful nature. There is a more fiendish and demonic power at work expressing itself from behind the scenes.

The Testimony of Scripture

More than such events themselves however, there is the witness of Scripture to the existence of Satan. In Scripture, Satan is mentioned directly more than 200 times. He is not seen as a simple personification of evil, but always as a real, spiritual being. The New Testament clearly testifies to and gives evidence of the existence of Satan and demons. When we examine Jesus' life and ministry in the Gospels we find that it is continually marked by encounters and confrontations with demons (Matt. 4:24; 8:16; Mk. 5:1-3; 9:25-27; Lk. 4:33-36). Jesus gave authority to His followers to cast out demons (Matt. 10:1,8; Lk. 10:17), and specific instances of this are recorded in the book of Acts (Acts 5;16; 8:6-8). The authority of Christians over demons is further supported by the teaching of the Early Church in the Epistles.

The existence of Satan and demons is clearly revealed in Scripture and upheld by our human experience throughout history. Let us now turn to Scripture to find out more about who Satan is.

Satan: Who is He?

In understanding who Satan is, it is essential that we recognize that he is not an eternal being who has always existed in opposition to God.

His Origin

The Bible tells us in Ezekiel 28:11-19, of a prophecy given against the King of Tyre, who is a type of Satan. Here we find that Satan was originally the highest angel of God's creation (Ezek. 28:14), "a model of perfection, full of wisdom and beauty" (Ezek. 28:12). Ezekiel goes on to say, "You were blameless in your ways from the day you were created till wickedness was found in you" (Ezek. 28:15). We see that God created Satan originally in perfection and blamelessness, and although He did not will evil in Satan, He did allow it. The evil that perverted Satan is described by Ezekiel, "Your heart became proud on account of your beauty, and you corrupted your wisdom because of your splendor" (Ezek. 28:17).

Another passage that gives more information on Satan's fall, is found in Isaiah. In words of lament he speaks, "How you have fallen from heaven, O morning star, son of the dawn! You have been cast down to the earth...You said in your heart, 'I will ascend to heaven...I will make myself like the Most High'" (Is. 14:12-14).

In selfish pride, Satan sought to rise above the sphere in which he was created, and above the purpose and service assigned to him. Not content to remain in the place God had given him, he wanted the supreme position and authority of God Himself. As a result, after this rebellion and attempt to usurp the place of God, who had created him, he was cast down to earth. In the beginning, God had created the beautiful Lucifer, meaning "morning star" or "light-bearer," to serve and love Him. Rejecting the honor God had given, he rebelled thus becoming Satan, meaning "adversary."

Who Satan is Not

As we have just seen from Scripture, Satan is a created being. This means that he is not an eternal being like God. He is not another omnipotent being equal to God, and opposite in nature. The Bible does not allow for any dualism such as is found in many other religions. C. S. Lewis points out, "Satan, the leader or dictator of devils, is the opposite not of God, but of Michael."[1]

Also, Satan is no god. Although Satan would like to be God (Is. 14:14) and be worshiped as God (Lk. 4:5-7), he is no more than one of God's creations. Although he is powerful, his power is not equal to God's. He is a finite creature and limited. Therefore, Satan is not omniscient, omnipotent, nor omnipresent. These are qualities that belong to God alone. He is ultimately subject to God and may do no more than God allows him to do. Perhaps a simple chart would help us to see these differences more clearly.

Contrast Between God and Satan		
Attributes	**God**	**Satan**
Being	not created, but the eternally existent, "I Am"	creature; created by God
Nature	holy; just; perfect; righteous	sinful; wicked; corrupt; evil
Actions in Relation to Humanity	to the ultimate good of humanity	to the destruction of humanity
Power	infinite; unlimited	finite; restricted

Chart 1

Satan: A Personal Being

The Bible speaks of the personality of Satan as fully as it speaks of any other personal being referred to in it. All the characteristics of personality are ascribed to Satan—he is referred to by personal pronouns; he is spoken of as having personal attributes: he has a will, he has knowledge, and there are personal acts performed by

---

[1] C. S. Lewis, *The Screwtape Letters* (New York: Macmillan, 1991), p. vii.

him. Michael Green has described his personality by saying: "he is an organizing intellect, a single focus and fount of evil inspiration."[2] He goes on to say that "he is an intelligence, a power of concentrated and hateful wickedness."[3] Satan is no myth, no figure of speech, nor merely a metaphorical personification of evil— he is a real, personal, spirit being.

Satan's Character and Nature

One of Satan's greatest assets, in opposing the work of the Lord, is his deceptiveness. He presents himself to people, posing so as to cause them to think of him in any way other than the way he truly is—his true character. However, the Bible refers to Satan by many different designations. These designations are descriptive of his character and reveal much about his true nature.[4]

Names of Satan

♦ **Beelzebub** (Matt. 12:24; 10:25): originally this signified "lord of the flies," Jews later changed it derisively to "lord of the dunghill." But the name is specifically given in Scripture to the "prince of demons."
♦ **Belial** (Deut. 13:13; Jdg. 20:13; 1 Sam. 10:27; 30:22): this means "good for nothing" or "the worthless one."
♦ **Devil**: this name means "Slanderer." See Accuser.
♦ **Lucifer** (Is. 14:12): this means "lightbearer," or "morning star." This name reminds us that he once occupied an exalted place

---

[2] Michael Green, *Exposing the Prince of Darkness* (Ann Arbor, MI: Servant Publications, 1981), p. 30.
[3] Ibid.
[4] The three categories of designations were taken from the study guide *Signs and Wonders* by Dr. Peter Prosser, 1993.

Biblical Designations for Satan		
Name	**Titles**	**Representations**
Beelzebub (Matt. 12:24; 10:25)	Accuser of the brethren (Rev. 12:10)	Angel of Light (2 Cor. 11:14)
Belial (Dt. 13:13; Jdg 20:13)	Deceiver (Rev. 12:9; 20:2,3,10)	Dragon (Rev. 12:3,7; 13:2)
Devil (slanderer, accuser)	god of the world (age) (2 Cor. 4:4)	Roaring Lion (1 Pet. 5:8)
Lucifer (Is. 14:12)	Liar, the Father of Lies (Jn. 8:44)	Serpent (Gen. 3:1ff, 2 Cor. 11:13; Rev. 12:9)
Satan (Adversary) (1 Pet. 5:8)	Murderer (Jn. 8:44)	
	Prince of the Power of the Air (Eph. 2:2)	
	Prince of this World (Jn.12:31; 14:30; 16:11)	
	Tempter (Matt. 4:3)	
	Thief (Jn.10:10)	
	Wicked (Evil) One (Matt 13:19; 1 Jn. 5:19)	

Chart 2

in heaven. It is important to remember then, that his appeal to us may at times seem high and lofty.

♦ **Satan** (1 Pet. 5:8): the meaning of this name is "Adversary." He is an opponent, the author of many malicious and persistent attempts to hinder God's program. He is opposed to everything and every one that is good.

Titles for Satan

♦ **Accuser of the Brethren** (Rev. 12:10): this comes from the term *diabolos* or "devil." He is a slanderer who brings accusations against us to condemn us.

- **Deceiver** (Rev. 20:10; 12:9; 20:2,3): this title is representative of one of the primary tactics of Satan, to deceive and cause people to believe that which is not true.
- **god of this World [Age]** (2 Cor. 4:4): this reference speaks of his prominence and rulership in the realm of religion. He seeks to distract people from seeing the true glory of God and promotes doctrines of demons. He seeks worship to glorify himself rather than God.
- **Liar, the Father of Lies** (Jn. 8:44): he is one in whom there is no truth, and not only does he deceive, but he lies blatantly. He is the author of lies and falsehood, especially "white lies" that have some kernel of truth in them, but are distorted.
- **Murderer** (Jn. 8:44): his twisted nature is to be a murderer, consistent with Jesus' description of him in John 10:10, "the thief comes only to kill, steal and destroy. . . " He is one who promotes sin which leads to death.
- **Prince of the Power of the Air** (Eph. 2:2): this may indicate that the sphere of Satan's activity is in the atmosphere around the earth. He is seen as being at the head of the "powers of this dark world and . . .the spiritual forces of evil in the heavenly realms" (Eph. 6:12). He has an evil empire over which he rules and though limited, is a power to be taken seriously.
- **Prince of this World** (Jn. 12:31; 14:30; 16:11): this speaks of Satan's relationship to the present world and particularly to his rule and influence over governments of this world. Much that happens in politics, business, and society are due to his influence. This dominion over the world was given to him when Adam forfeited his right in the garden. He may be "prince," but he is not "king." Ultimately, he is still subject to the Lord Jesus Christ.

♦ **Tempter** (Matt. 4:3): Satan tempts people for the purpose of destroying them. He incites them to evil in order to alienate them from God.

♦ **Thief** (Jn. 10:10): he is here described as one who seeks to take what is not his and "to kill, steal, and destroy."

♦ **Wicked (Evil) One** (Matt. 13:19; 1 Jn. 5:19): Satan is the embodiment of disobedience and lawlessness and evil to the core.

Representations of Satan

♦ **Angel of Light** (2 Cor. 11:14): this is consistent with his former position and title of "lightbearer." Satan is a fallen angelic being and may deceptively disguise himself as a messenger of "light," but there is no light in him, only darkness.

♦ **Dragon** (Rev. 12:3,7; 13:2): literally this means "sea monster," but it pictures the power, fierceness, and the fearsomeness of this enemy. "Many ancient religions saw the dragon as the pristine foe of all that is good...It was one of the traditional ways of conceiving of the spirit of evil throughout the near East; a monstrous beast, wreaking havoc and destruction on the earth, and devouring man."[5]

♦ **Roaring Lion** (1 Pet. 5:8): note that he is not described as a roaring lion, but "like" a roaring lion. Nevertheless, he roams around seeking unaware prey that he may devour. He projects fierceness and strength.

♦ **Serpent** (Gen. 3:1ff; 2 Cor. 11:3; Rev. 12:9): this is the first biblical title given to Satan. It denotes particularly his crookedness, deceitfulness, craftiness, and guile. And just as the bite of a venomous snake may be deadly to the body, so the

---

[5] Green, p. 44.

words of Satan, "the serpent" are poisonous to the soul and spirit of humankind.

Satan's Work

There are many ways in which Satan works in the world and in the lives of men and women. Some of these have been seen in the various designations that we have just looked at. However, Scripture gives further light on his specific activities among humanity in general and among Christians in particular.

Among Humanity in General

- ♦ He is the author of sin and continues to tempt people to sin (Gen. 3:1-6).
- ♦ He holds the power of death as a threat and keeps people in bondage to the fear of death (Heb. 2:14).
- ♦ He seeks to take away the Word of God from the hearts of people so that they may not believe and be saved (Lk. 8:12).
- ♦ He can cause sickness and suffering (Acts 10:38), although not all sickness and suffering can be attributed to him.
- ♦ He can personally enter and control a person as he did Judas (Jn. 13:27).
- ♦ He blinds people's minds so that they may not see the truth of the gospel (2 Cor. 4:4).
- ♦ He encourages and inspires false religions and spirituality referred to by Paul as "doctrines of demons" (1 Tim. 4:1-3).

Among Christians in Particular

- ♦ He sets traps and snares to cause believers to fall into sin and disgrace, destroying their testimony (1 Tim. 3:7).
- ♦ He accuses and slanders believers to bring them under condemnation and to attempt to bring them under God's wrath (Rev. 12:10).

♦ He can place wicked thoughts and plans into the minds of people, inspiring all forms of evil (Jn. 13:2; Acts 5:3).

♦ He attempts to oppose and harass God's servants (Lk. 22:31; 2 Cor. 12:7).

♦ He hinders the work of God's servants (1 Thes. 2:18).

♦ He incites persecution against believers (Rev. 2:10).

♦ He orchestrates the work of demons in an attempt to defeat believers (Eph. 6:11-12).

♦ He tempts believers to engage in immorality (1 Cor. 7:5).

Demons: Who Are They?

The Bible may not tell us all we want to know about the subject of demons, but all that God has deemed necessary for us to know is revealed to us.

Origin

There have been different theories of varying credibility proposed to account for the origin of demons.

Theory #1: Demons are created beings. This is not a theory which is commonly proposed, but it is a position that must be dealt with at the outset. This view would hold that demons are a specific order of created beings. The Bible makes no allowance for this view whatsoever. Demons in the Scriptures are clearly and consistently depicted as evil and in opposition to God and people, and operate under the authority of Satan.

The Scripture is equally clear that when God created the universe and all the creatures that are in it, He pronounced that "it was very good" (Gen. 1:31). It is impossible then, that God could have created any creature that was in its very nature, evil. Whatever else might be said about the origin of demons, must be with the understanding that they are an order of spiritual beings who, when they were created, were good but fell and became corrupted. There is no scriptural support for a view that sees demons as a special creation of God.

Theory #2: Demons are the disembodied spirits of a pre-Adamic race of humans. This view holds that Genesis 1:1 refers to the creation of a perfect earth and that somewhere between Genesis 1:1 and Genesis 1:2 there is a great gap in time. During this time, it is said that the world and a pre-Adamic race of humans, was ruled over by Satan, in his unfallen state as Lucifer. In the angelic rebellion of Lucifer and other angels (Isaiah 14:12-14), these pre-Adamic people were somehow involved. Due to this rebellion, God brought judgment upon them all resulting in a worldwide catastrophe. In the process, the spirits of these humans were separated from their bodies. In Genesis 1:3, God begins to recreate order from the chaos and in this recreation these disembodied spirits became what we know today as demons.

This view rests primarily on reading the phrase in Genesis 1:2, "And the earth *was* formless and void..." as "And the earth *became* formless and void..." (emphasis added) C. Fred Dickason notes "that it is doubtful that the verb in verse 2 could be translated 'became,'" and that Hebrew scholars find very little support for the gap theory in the words or grammar used.[6] Also, if one were to allow this gap and the supposed pre-Adamic race, there is no scriptural evidence to link the spirits of this race to demons. Most of the evidence for this view is highly conjectural and reads a lot into the supposed gap between Genesis 1:1 and 1:2.

Theory #3: Demons are the illicit offspring of angels and women. Another theory given to explain the origin of demons is

---

[6] C. Fred Dickason, *Angels, Elect and Evil* (Chicago: Moody Press, 1975), p. 156.

based on the text of Genesis 6:1-4. This view holds that the "sons of God" mentioned in this text were angels who defied God's natural order and had sexual relations with women. The heinous nature of this sin provoked God's wrath and He sent the flood in judgment. Although the bodies of the unnatural offspring of these angelic and human unions were destroyed, their disembodied spirits remained and became demons.

To support this view, reference is made to Jude 6, which speaks of "angels that did not keep their own position but left their proper dwelling" (RSV). The sin of these angels is thereby identified by the context as sexual immorality and further explained as indulging in unnatural lust,[7] a perversion of God's natural order. Also, both in Genesis 6 and 2 Peter 2:4-6, the fuller context of this great sin connects it closely with God's judgment and the flood.[8]

The use of the exact term, "sons of God" in Hebrew, is used apart from Genesis 6 only in reference to angels.[9] To use it in Genesis 6 to refer to human beings would not be entirely consistent. However, if the "sons of God" does refer to fallen angels, there is no other biblical evidence to show that the offspring of this union should be identified as demons. Some have stated instead, that the term "sons of God" does not refer to angels, but to men, descendants of Seth, who intermarried with women who were descendants of Cain (Gen. 4,5).

In the Bible, angels seem to have been created as a complete host, fixed in number with no procreation, and therefore with no need for sexual characteristics. At the same time, we should note

---

[7] The angels who engaged in these unnatural acts are now, "kept by him in eternal chains in the nether gloom until the judgment of the great day" (Jude 6).

[8] Dickason, p. 224.

[9] Ibid., p. 223.

Theories of the Origin of Demons

	Theory #1	Theory #2	Theory #3	Theory #4
Theory Stated:	Demons are a specific order of beings created by God.	Demons are the disembodied spirits of a now destroyed pre-Adamic race of humans.	Demons are the illicit offspring of angels and women.	Demons are "fallen angels"—a host of angels who rebelled against God and were cast down from heaven.
Main Support	None	◆ there is a possible gap in time between Gen. 1:1 and 1:2 ◆ Gen. 1:2 should read, "And the earth *became* formless and void…" ◆ a pre-Adamic race of people lived during a time before Gen. 1:2	◆ interprets "sons of God" in Gen. 6:1-4 as angels ◆ believes Jude 6 refers to these errant angels ◆ Gen. 6 and 2 Pet. 2:4-6 place the sin of these angels in the context of the judgment of the flood ◆ angels could take on human form and thereby have sexual relations with women	◆ biblical texts which seem to identify fallen angels with demons (Matt. 25:41; Rev. 12:7; Matt. 12:24,26) ◆ Satan appears to be identified as a demon—"ruler of the demons" ◆ angels and demons are similar in being and activities ◆ similar rankings among angels and demons

Counter-arguments	◆ all that God created was good (Gen. 1:31) ◆ God created no evil; therefore could not have created demons	◆ unlikely that verb in Gen. 1:2 could be translated "became"; it should read "was" ◆ little grammatical support for the supposed "gap" between Gen. 1:1 and 1:2 ◆ no biblical evidence of a pre-Adamic race; it is pure conjecture	◆ the term "sons of God" does not refer to angels but to the godly line of Seth ◆ angels are neither male nor female; they are nonsexual beings and could not have sexual relations with women ◆ the supposition that the offspring of fallen angels and women became demons is speculation and not explicit in Scripture	◆ if Jude 6-7 and 2 Pet. 2:4-6 refer to the original fall of these angels, then they would be bound and not able to freely roam as demons ◆ some apparent differences between angels and demons—angels able to take on human form; demons entered humans ◆ that angels and demons are both referred to as "spirits" is not conclusive that they are the same; humans too, are living spirit beings
Conclusion	Not possible	Not possible; pure conjecture	Possible, though unlikely	Most likely, though not certain

Chart 3

that in Scripture, angels can take on human form and appearance so that people are not able to distinguish them as angels. In cases where angels appeared as human, they seem to be consistently identified as male. J. Rodman Williams affirms that "angels are neither male nor female: they are nonsexual"[10] Their nature as nonsexual and spiritual beings, would then mean that they could not have had sexual relations with women.

However, although the Bible does say that in heaven we will be like the angels (Matt. 22:30), it does not explicitly say that angels are sexless creatures. Furthermore, since godly angels, when taking on human form, engaged in human activities such as talking and eating, there is nothing to suggest that fallen angels could not similarly have taken on human form with sexual features and functions.

And so, although there may have been sexual contact between these fallen angels and antediluvian women, the supposition that their offspring became disembodied spirits or demons is as Merrill F. Unger says, "pure speculation...the fate of their mongrel offspring is not told in Scripture."[11]

Theory #4: Demons are fallen angels. It is held in this theory that when Satan exalted himself and rebelled against God (Is. 14:12-14; Ezek. 28:2-19), he was joined by a large number of other angelic beings, perhaps up to a third of all of them (Rev. 12:4). These rebellious angels were cast down from heaven and became what we now call demons. There appears to be two classes, those that are free and those that are confined. This is probably the most

[10] Williams, *Renewal Theology*, Vol. 1, p. 178.
[11] Merrill F. Unger, *Demons in the World Today* (Wheaton, IL: Tyndale House Publishers, 1971), p. 15.
[12] The five points are taken from C. Fred Dickason, *Demon Possession & the Christian* (Chicago, IL: Moody Press, 1987), pp. 24-25.

widely accepted explanation for the origin of demons. Dickason, representing this view, lists five reasons in support of this theory:[12]

1) Demons have a relation to Satan that is similar to Satan's angels. In biblical references to Satan and his hosts, there are parallel expressions which would seem to identify fallen angels and demons: "the devil and his angels" (Matt. 25:41); "the dragon and his angels" (Rev. 12:7); "Beelzebub, the ruler of the demons" (Matt. 12:24,26)[13]

2) Satan himself seems to be identified not only as a fallen angel, but as a demon. In the text where Satan is called the "ruler of the demons," the word used is *archonti*. The basic meaning of this is "first." And so, "as first among the demons, he is their ruler."[14]

3) Both demons and angels are similar in their being. Angels are referred to as "spirits" (Ps. 104:4; Heb. 1:14), as likewise are demons (Matt. 8:16; Lk. 10:17-20).

4) Demons and evil angels are also involved in the same kinds of activities. Demons desire to enter into people and exercise control over them (Matt. 17:14-18; Lk. 11;14-15). The same is true of evil angels, like Satan (Lk. 22:3; Jn. 13:27). Both evil angels and demons are similarly said to join Satan in his warfare against God and humankind (Rev. 12:7-17; Mk. 9:17-26; Rev. 9:13-15).

5) Scripture sets forth rankings and variety among both angels and demons that are parallel in nature. This would seem to indicate that angels and demons are similar, if not identical (Rom. 8:38-39; Eph. 6:10-12; Col. 1:16; 2:15).

---

[13] Beelzebub was the name of a Canaanite deity that the Jews used to denote Satan.

[14] Charles R. Smith, "The New Testament Doctrine of Demons," *Grace Journal 10* (Spring 1969): p. 32; quoted in C. Fred Dickason, *Demon Possession & the Christian: A New Perspective* (Chicago: Moody Press, 1987), p. 24, n.4.

Which Theory of Origins?

Having looked at the different views on the origin of demons we have to say that the Bible does not tell us all we might want to know and is silent on their precise origin. I personally tend to hold to the fourth theory, that demons are fallen angels, primarily because it seems to have more scriptural and rational support and is the position of the majority of evangelical scholars.[15] Fortunately, even though we cannot know with certainty the origin of demons, we can know their ultimate fate and participate with Christ in His victory over all the spiritual hosts of wickedness.

The Nature and Activity of Demons

The name "demon" comes from the Latin *daemon*, meaning evil spirit, and from the Greek *daimon*, meaning divinity. It is applied in the Bible to angels who were once perfect, sinless beings, who sinned (probably joining in with Lucifer's revolt) and were cast down to earth or into hell and are now under Satan's direction. C. S. Lewis writes, "They do not differ in nature from good angels, but their nature is depraved."[16]

There appear to be two classes of demons – those confined, perhaps because they are too harmful or dangerous to be allowed to roam the earth; and those allowed to move about freely on the earth and in some way serve Satan. Of those that are confined, some are bound in *tartarus*, the nether gloom, as the result of some terrible sin and are awaiting the final judgment (Jude 6-7; 2 Pet.

---

[15] Though this is the position that will be taken throughout the remainder of this book, it is a view which is held lightly and not dogmatically. The third theory seems to hold some merit and cannot be entirely dismissed. See the discussion by Clinton E. Arnold, *Powers of Darkness* (Downers Grove, IL: Intervarsity Press, 1992), pp. 65-67.

[16] Lewis.

2:4-6). Other of these evil angels are confined for a season to the abyss [or bottomless pit] (Lk. 8:31; Rev. 9:1-3,11) and will be released during the Tribulation to afflict the wicked (Rev. 9:1-21; 16:13-14). The other class of fallen angels are those which are free to roam as demons under Satan's authority and carry on his work (Eph. 6:11-12) in warfare against good angels and believers upon the earth.[17]

Demons were created originally by God as angels at the beginning of time and they don't die. They are spirit beings, personalities without physical bodies, often referred to in the Bible as "evil spirits" (Lk. 4:33; 8:29; 9:42). They are intelligent creatures and although they are far from having all knowledge [omniscience], their wisdom and knowledge exceeds that of humans (Acts 19:15; Jas. 2:19). They are clever, crafty, and cunning [after all they have thousands of years of experience in deceit]. They attempt to interfere with the fulfillment of God's purposes (Dan. 10:10-13; Rev. 16:13-16), yet they may ultimately be used by God in His sovereignty to carry out His purposes (1 Sam. 16:14; 2 Cor. 12:7). They recognize Jesus (Mk. 1:24) and must submit to His authority (Mk. 5:7-13; Lk. 8:26-33), and they know their own fate (Matt. 8:29; Mk. 1:24).

Demons are numerous [perhaps as many as 1/3 of all the original angels] (Rev. 12:7-12). They are well organized into what appears to be a hierarchy of differing ranks (Eph. 6:12). These rankings of demons seem to vary in power and authority (Dan. 10:13,20,21; 12;1) and in their degree of malevolent wickedness (Matt. 8:28; 12:43-45; Mk. 9:29).

Demons are also cunningly deceptive. The word "demon" conjures up in our imagination images of grotesque, distorted, and dis-

---

[17] Dickason, *Angels, Elect and Evil*, p. 158.

figured creatures. But all demons don't look like demons. Remember they are actually fallen angels and may appear as "angels of light." In other words, they may seem to be attractive, benign beings. Much modern noninstitutional spirituality has taken a renewed interest in angels and accept them all without discerning their true nature. It was an angel calling itself "Moroni" that appeared to Joseph Smith, leading him into founding a new pseudo-Christian cult called Mormonism. These so-called angelic messengers bring false teachings (1 Tim. 4:1-3) to deceive and lead astray. Paul warned the Galatians saying that, "...even if we or an angel from heaven should preach a gospel other than the one we preached to you, let him be eternally condemned" (Gal. 1:8).

The earth and the air are demons' sphere of activity (Eph. 2:2; 6:12), yet much of their activity is directed toward humanity. It seems that they desire to inhabit people's bodies, and in this way they can manifest and express themselves. The New Testament is clear in revealing that they can enter into people (Matt. 4:24), speak through them (Mk. 5:7-10), give them superhuman strength (Mk. 5:2-4; Acts 19:13-16), and afflict them with disease or other infirmities (Matt. 9:32-33; Lk. 13:11). However, they may also enter into animals (Mk. 5:13). It would appear that demons may also inhabit a place (Dan. 10:13; Rev. 2:13; 18:2) or attach themselves to an object, particularly one used for occult or false religious purposes. Idolatrous objects are connected with the presence and activity of demons. In 1 Corinthians 10:19-20, Paul recognizes that idols in themselves are nothing (see also Ps. 135:15-17; 106:36-37), but that demons are connected with them. Lester Sumrall gives an illuminating account from a trip to China:

> I visited a large Buddhist temple where the priests showed
> me their gods, many of which were ugly, frightening idols

with eight or ten arms. Pointing to one about 16 feet high, I asked the priest, "How can that idol help you?" He was very polite. "You don't understand, being a foreigner," he said. "That idol does not have power. We all know that. The spirit of that idol is elsewhere right now, but if I were to bring incense and food and place it before that idol, something would start happening." Then he took me to the rear of the idol and pointed to a hole. "That's where the spirit goes in and out," he said. "It wants worship. If I come and kneel here and offer an offering and burn incense or candles, immediately the spirit comes and communicates with me."[18]

Demons in Cultural Context

As was mentioned, the Bible indicates that demons are of differing ranks and vary in their power, authority, and degree of wickedness. But how is it that they manifest themselves; how do they make themselves known? In the Philippines, where we served as missionaries for ten years, there was much from the pre-Christian beliefs that carried into the folk religious beliefs of today, particularly regarding various beings from the spirit-world.

In the pre-Christian belief system of the Filipino, there were various classes (rankings) of spirit-beings. There were for example the *anito*, (intermediate) deities that were involved in the affairs of everyday life. They lived in trees, caves, and rivers. The *anito* were placated by the offering of sacrifices in various forms, often performed by a spiritual practitioner. There were also ancestral spirits—the spirits of departed members of the family, village, or

---

[18] Lester Sumrall, *Demons: The Answer Book* (South Bend, IN: LeSEA Publishing Co., 1979), p. 115.

tribe. These too, had to be remembered and honored through prayer and sacrifice. There were also other spirit-beings such as the *duwende* (dwarfs), *kapre* (ogres), *aswang* (vampires), and others.[19]

These beliefs about supernatural spirit-beings are not unlike those held by other people groups around the world. In the Western world there are all kinds of folk legends derived from different European cultures that speak of creatures that are half-gods and half-men, of trolls, ogres, goblins, brownies, elves, leprechauns, werewolves, vampires, of water spirits and tree spirits. Many modern holiday celebrations and their customs trace their roots back to these legends and creatures. Although the legends that have grown up around these beings may have been greatly exaggerated over time, there is probably some basis in fact.

How are these various creatures and their activities to be explained? Considering the Bible's teaching on the spirit-world, they may best be understood as the visible manifestations of what the Bible refers to as demons, interfering in and trying to manipulate the lives of men and women down through the ages. They certainly fit the biblical characteristics of evil spirits. If this is so, then there is worldwide historical and cultural evidence of the widespread activity of the demonic in the lives of many people, which continues even today.

Whatever form they may take, demons are at enmity with God and with humanity, desiring to keep people enslaved and separated from a true knowledge of God. Yet Jesus Christ is Lord over all the spirit-world and those who will acknowledge Him as Savior may experience complete freedom and victory over these powers of darkness.

---

[19] Rodney L. Henry, *Filipino Spirit World* (Manila: OMF Publishers, 1986).

The Defeat of Satan and Demons

It is important that we not underestimate our enemy. He is a potent and vicious adversary; nevertheless, his power is limited. Although he and his demonic legion can hinder the progress of God's work in the world, they cannot prevent it. Scripture affirms that Satan's defeat is assured and his final destiny already determined. Consider these statements:

- ◆ He was cast out of his original, exalted position in heaven (Is. 14:15; Ezek. 28:16).
- ◆ He was cursed in the garden of Eden (Gen. 3:14-15).
- ◆ He was defeated by Christ in the wilderness temptation (Matt. 4:3-11).
- ◆ He was judged at the cross of Calvary (Jn. 12:31; Heb. 2:14; Col. 2:15).
- ◆ He is to be confined in the Abyss during the Millennium (Rev. 20:2).
- ◆ He will ultimately be consigned to the Lake of Fire for eternity (Rev. 20:10).

Jesus Christ has already won the victory over Satan (Matt. 4:1-11; Rom. 5:12-19; Col. 2:13-15). And we who are in Christ participate in that victory (Eph. 1:19-23), being seated with Him in heavenly places over all evil authorities. Through the salvation God has provided us in Jesus Christ, we are set free from Satan's domination (Acts 26:18; Col. 1:13-14). Therefore, although we need to respect the formidable power of our enemies, we do not need to fear them. As we take our stand in Christ, we will see them overcome.

Chapter Three

How Demons
Affect People

Scripture doesn't give a complete list of the ways evil spirits affect people. The main intention of the gospel writers was not to present us with a catalogue of all the activities of evil spirits, but rather to show that Jesus overcame the kingdom of Satan and exercised authority over them no matter where He found them. Nevertheless, the encounters of Jesus with Satan and evil spirits do give us a picture of the ways the forces of evil operate in this world.

We need to be aware that the kingdom of Satan is powerful and well-organized and it can affect people in many ways. Many people experience spiritual, mental, and physical problems and never seem to find real healing through the normal medical means. It is quite possible that demons may be the cause of these problems. This book is not aimed at dealing with all the aspects of spiritual warfare—but rather with looking particularly at the ways in which participation in the occult may bring a person under some form of bondage to evil spirits and then to present a means of being freed from that bondage through Jesus Christ.

Demonic Activity

Various systems have been used to describe demonic activity toward people. One helpful way has been suggested by John Wimber who views demonic attacks in three primary areas: temptation, opposition, and demonization.[1] I have found it helpful to view these on a spectrum as pictured in the chart below:

Spectrum of Demonic Activity				
External Interference		**Internal Influence**		
Temptation	Opposition	Demonic Entry	Partial Demonic Control	Severe Demonization

Chart 4

External Interference

Evil spirits attack people in every way conceivable. These attacks may come from the outside, or from the inside of a person. Temptation and opposition are two forms of demonic activity directed against people from the outside.

Temptation

"Scripture sometimes talks about the struggle between the spirit and the flesh (i.e., sinful nature) (Gal. 5:17), and in other instances speaks of Satan tempting men and women (1 Thes. 3:5). These two influences often work together: the flesh opens us to satanic influence, and Satan is the author of temptation."[2] We face many temptations in the course of our day-to-day lives. Most of these could be regarded as the result of our own desires, the decisions we

---

[1]   John Wimber, *Power Healing* (San Francisco, CA: Harper & Row, 1987), p. 106.
[2]   Ibid.

make, and the influence that the world has on us. But in addition, there is a kind of temptation that may involve more direct demonic influence.

Satan appears as the tempter at the very beginning of the human story. Through his seductions, Adam and Eve sinned and turned from God. This is Satan's basic purpose in temptation—to entice people to sin in order to hinder, block, and ultimately to sever their relationship with God. This was his objective with Job. Satan wanted to put the kind of pressure on Job that would lead him to "curse God and die." In the New Testament we find that Satan tempted Jesus when He was in the wilderness and he also tempted Ananias to lie about the money he gave to aid others in the church.

The purpose of all satanic temptation is to lead people away from God. Satan's temptations are as numerous and varied as a person's capacity for sin. He tailors his attacks to fit each individual's own particular set of weaknesses. Demonic temptations can take place at various levels. They can range from simple and everyday temptations to bizarre thoughts and expressions. The temptations encompass everything from "little white lies" to murder and adultery.

The occult promises of secret knowledge, supernatural power, and control are particularly attractive to many people. Evil spirits seek out opportunities to use one's natural weaknesses to their own advantage. Keeping a close watch on a person's spiritual, physical, and emotional weak points, they look for occasions to strike and inflict whatever damage they can; and they'll persist in their attacks on an area of this person's life as long as they remain unchallenged.

Demonic temptation can be very subtle and often unnoticeable, yet there are some characteristics of this type of demonic activity. When the temptation is of an urgent, insistent, or

overwhelming quality, when the temptation is of a strongly compulsive nature, or when it is long standing and habitual, it is highly
possible that evil spirits are at work. The world, the flesh, and the
devil are all working together to tempt us, to keep us off guard, to
trap us in sin, and ultimately to ensure our death.

To be tempted, whether by your sinful flesh or a demonic agent,
is no sin in itself. Temptation is common to all men and women.
Even Jesus Himself was tempted (Lk. 4:1-13; Heb. 4:15-16). To
encounter temptation is a natural occurrence. Yet each person is
responsible for how they respond to those temptations. To yield to
temptation, to give in and act on the temptation—that is sin. And
as Wimber notes, "When we yield to the temptations of the flesh
and the world, we become more vulnerable to further demonic temptation. . .the more we sin, the more susceptible we are to demonic
temptation."[3]

The more often one gives in to temptation, the stronger the
grip of temptation is in that particular area of life and the greater
the opportunity for demons to exploit the weakness and bring you
under further bondage. This is clearly evident in the lives of those
who surrender to the lure of the occult. Yet, the call of God to us is
to resist the temptation, to simply say "no." For the Christian, God
will provide the power and the grace to resist (1 Cor 10:13). And
as we resist temptation, both the hold of sin and demonic powers
will be weakened.

Opposition

Satan and his evil spirits also attack humankind in general and
Christians in particular by trying to prevent the preaching of the
gospel and the spreading of the kingdom of God. In the lives of

---

[3]   Wimber., p. 107.

individuals, demons will attempt to block a person's coming to the Lord or growing in a deeper relationship with the Lord.

"The job of demons is to hinder good by any possible means. Demons try to keep people from God or from doing anything God wants. They hinder unbelievers from believing (2 Cor. 4:4). They also work to undermine the faith of Christians. Worship, prayer, Bible study, expressions of love, and acts of compassion are high on the demonic hit list."[4]

An instance in the book of Acts may help to illustrate this. Barnabas and Saul were visiting in Paphos and were invited by the proconsul to come and share the word of God with him. But one of his aids was a sorcerer and false prophet, named Elymas. This sorcerer opposed the preaching of Barnabas and Saul and tried to turn the proconsul away from faith in God. "Then Saul, who was also called Paul, filled with the Holy Spirit, looked straight at Elymas and said, 'You are a child of the devil and an enemy of everything that is right! You are full of all kinds of deceit and trickery. Will you never stop perverting the right ways of the Lord?'" (Acts 13:8-10).

In this case, the opposition to the gospel was clearly inspired by demonic forces working through a man deeply involved in the occult. Nevertheless, Barnabas and Saul knew how to respond in the power of the Holy Spirit, Elymas' interference was dealt with, and the proconsul turned to Christ. However, this account points out the reality of demonic opposition.

Opposition can take many forms. Demonic opposition will entice some to leave the truth of Christianity for lies, encourage religiosity through formalism, legalism, or asceticism, or promote

---

[4]   Charles H. Kraft, *Defeating Dark Angels* (Ann Arbor, MI: Servant Publications, 1992), p. 107.

idolatry. Opposition also means demonic harassment. "We can assume demons are involved in every kind of disruption ... [They] push, prod, tempt, and entice to get people to make bad or at least unwise decisions. And when they find someone already in difficulty, they work to make it worse."[5] Demons will use any means at their disposal to try to hinder good relationships between people. Opposition may also come through accidents, the counterfeiting of supernatural gifts, or even making someone sick.

Charles Kraft has said, "I don't know how much power demons have over the ordinary circumstances of life. But I would wager that they do whatever God allows to disrupt our lives through influencing such things as traffic, weather, health, stress, relationships, worship, sleep, diet, and machines (especially cars and computers)."[6] Demonic interference is not always the cause of things going wrong—but when it is the cause, then things will not go right until we directly confront the evil spirits in the power of the Holy Spirit and the name of Jesus Christ.

Internal Influence

A third way in which demons affect people is through demonization. While other ways demons affect people are external, from without, in demonization, people are affected from within. Also, temptation and opposition are common to everyone, however that is not true with demonization. Only some people are demonized— those in which evil spirits have gained entry.

Demonization

Although most translations of the Bible speak of "demon possession," this is *not* the meaning of the term actually used. In the

---

[5] Kraft, p. 102.
[6] Ibid., p. 110.

Greek, the word is *daimonizomai*, and it refers to the involvement of demons or a demon-caused passivity. Rather than speaking of demon possession, a better way to speak of it is to say that a person is "demonized." Demon possession implies ownership, but demons can't really own anything. Rather, they are trespassers or squatters, intruding on territory that is not their own.

I believe John Wimber has made an accurate assessment when he says, "I do not believe that demons may own people absolutely while they still live on earth; even when demons gain a high degree of control, people are able to exercise a degree of free will."[7] There are also other parallel expressions to "demonized," that speak of a person "*having* a demon" (Lk. 4:33), or "a man *with* an unclean spirit" (Mk. 1:23), or someone being "*afflicted with* unclean spirits" (Acts 5:16). These all speak of the internal presence and activity of evil spirits in someone, but none of these indicate the idea of "possession."

What happens in demonization is that demons gain entrance to men and women and attack them by getting a grip on their personalities or physical lives. C. Fred Dickason has developed a very helpful definition of demonization, "...we may define demonization as demon-caused passivity or control due to a demon's residing within a person, which manifests its effects in various physical and mental disorders and in varying degrees."[8] These varying degrees of demonization may be said to range from mild to severe, depending on the severity of the effects and the apparent extent of control exercised.

There are two factors which seem affect the severity of the demonization. First, the degree of wickedness of the evil spirit.

---

[7] Wimber, p. 109.

[8] C. Fred Dickason, *Demon Possession and the Christian* (Westchester, IL: Crossway Books, 1990), p. 40.

Apparently, some demons are more powerful or more wicked than others (Matt. 12:44-45). The second factor is the number of evil spirits inhabiting a person. Since spirit-beings are not limited by physical space, there may be more than one inhabiting the same person (Mk. 5:9-13; Lk. 8:2). It would seem to follow that the more demons present, the stronger their hold over their victim. Because of the degree of direct demonic activity in the occult, it is not uncommon for those who participate in occultism to have some degree of demonization.

Can a Christian be Demonized?

There has been much debate over whether or not Christians can be demonized. A careful study of Scripture shows that one cannot prove conclusively one way or the other whether Christians can be demonized. The arguments against the possibility of Christians being demonized are, however, very weak.[9] Even those who from a theoretical position once believed that Christians could not be demonized, have changed their position once they have had actual experience in ministering to people who were demonized.[10] Merrill F. Unger, for instance, who once took a negative position now states that, "Clinical evidence abounds that a Christian can be demonized as a carry-over from pre-conversion days or can fall under Satan's power after conversion and become progressively demonized, even seriously."[11]

---

[9] An excellent and detailed discussion regarding the Christian and demon possession can be found in chapter two of the book by Clinton E. Arnold, *Three Crucial Questions about Spiritual Warfare* (Grand Rapids, MI: Baker Books, 1997).

[10] Among these are such noted ministers and counselors as Kurt Koch, Merrill F. Unger, Charles Swindoll, Charles H. Kraft, C. Fred Dickason, Ed Murphy, and C. Peter Wagner.

[11] Merrill F. Unger, *What Demons Can Do To Saints* (Chicago, IL: Moody Press, 1977), p. 137.

In evaluating what many Christian counselors have written on the subject, Kraft says, "...those with 'clinical' experience with Christians having demonic symptoms have overcome their doubts and concluded that Christians can and regularly do carry demons. They have also discovered that the power of Christ can break the demons' power."[12]

Most Christians who have experienced being demonized, were demonized before they became Christians and carried that over with them into their Christian life. However, it is also possible, though unusual, for a person who is a Christian to become demonized. In such cases, it is usually due to the Christian walking persistently in some area of sin which then opens a door for demonic entrance.

In discussing the possibility of a Christian being demonized, Dickason says, "None of the passages we have studied with any fair treatment can be construed to eliminate the possibility of a genuine believer's being inhabited by wicked spirits... We may say definitely, however, that the believer who heeds the warnings and obeys the Scripture and walks in fellowship with Christ cannot be freshly invaded."[13] The Christian who is living in right relationship with the Lord has no need to fear new demonic invasion.

The fact that a Christian is demonized will certainly affect the quality of his or her Christian life and the demonic presence will definitely have to be dealt with. However it is also important to affirm that a Christian being demonized does not affect or negate their salvation. "It must be stressed that demons cannot indwell a Christian in the same sense the Holy Spirit indwells. God's Spirit enters a believer at salvation, permanently, never to leave (Jn. 14:16). A demon, by contrast, enters as a squatter and an intruder, and is

---

[12] Kraft, p. 65.
[13] Dickason, p. 99.

subject to momentary eviction. A demon never rightfully or permanently indwells a saint (Christian believer), as the Holy Spirit does, and no demon can ever have influence over any part of a Christian's life that is yielded to the Holy Spirit."[14] When people have given their lives to Christ, they have been born again and Christ comes to live within them as the Lord of their lives. Their spirits have been made alive. They have been transferred from the kingdom of darkness to the kingdom of God. They belong to God, having been purchased by the blood of Christ.

Even though believers are cleansed from sin and delivered from its power, they still have to continually appropriate Christ's power to resist it and overcome it. Similarly, for the Christian who has been demonized, Christ's power must be appropriated so that any evil spirits resident in his or her life will be conquered and evicted.

Demonic Access through Occultism

Demons are able to gain access to people's lives through a variety of ways. But our concern here is primarily with the occult. As will become clear in the succeeding chapters, the Bible clearly warns against the dangers of occult involvement, for the occult is the special realm of operation of satanic and demonic power. So direct involvement with the occult is an open door of invitation to evil spirits. We cannot presume that everyone who has been involved with the occult is thereby demonized, but through ministry with those who have been demonized, the occult has been identified as one of the primary routes of demonic access to a person's life.

But even if a person has not been directly involved in the occult, it is possible that their parents, or other ancestors were involved in some form of occultism or even exercised some alleged

---

[14] Unger, pp. 51-52.

supernatural powers. It is possible that as a result of their participating in the occult, curses and evil spirits can be passed on to following generations. In Exodus, this warning is given, "I the Lord your God, am a jealous God, punishing the children for the sin of the fathers to the third and fourth generation of those who hate me." (Ex. 20:5) While this does not mean that demons are *always* passed from one generation to another, they *may* be. Occult powers, which have their source in demons, may also be passed on from one generation to the next.

Curses are another avenue by which demons may gain access to someone's life. Curses may simply be hurtful, derogatory words spoken against someone by their relatives or friends, or they may also be specific occult spells cast by magic ritual. Although curses seem to exercise a more external influence on people, they, along with other factors, may cause someone to eventually become demonized. This seems to be particularly true about non-Christians. It becomes evident then, that the occult in its various dimensions, provides a path of entry for evil spirits into people's lives.

Part Two

Occultism:
Satan's Trap Exposed

Chapter Four

Occultism

What Is Meant By "Occult"?

O ccult is a term that refers to a wide range of practices, beliefs, and phenomena, which are beyond the realm of empirical, scientific knowledge. There are three distinct characteristics of the occult: 1) it deals with things hidden or secret, 2) it deals with operations or events which seem to depend on human powers that go beyond the five senses, and 3) it deals with the supernatural, the presence of angelic or demonic forces.[1]

Almost all practices and objects associated with the occult can be classified under one of three main categories: 1) divination, 2) magic, or 3) spiritism. All of these forms of the occult are inter-related and there is some overlap between them. The occult is a primary instrument of Satan to deceive people and turn them away from God.

---

[1] David W. Hoover, *How to Respond to the Occult* (St. Louis, MO: Concordia Publishing House, 1977), p. 8.

Main Categories of Occult Practice		
Divination (fortune-telling)	**Magic** (sorcery)	**Spiritism** (necromancy)
Seeking supernatural guidance or knowledge apart from God or the means He has given.	The attempt to exercise control over people, nature, and one's environment through supernatural means.	The attempt to gain secret knowledge or power through communication with the dead or other spirit beings.

Chart 5

Scripture speaks to us often of Christ who has come as a light to reveal what is hidden in darkness. There is a great need to expose and bring the darkness of occultism into the light. We often fear what we don't know or can't see. As long as something remains unknown, all kinds of myths and stories can be created about it to keep it shrouded in mystery. However, when the true nature of that which has been hidden in darkness is made known and we see it for what it truly is, the surrounding mystery is dispelled along with the fear that often accompanies it.

This is true of Satan's field of operation in the occult. There is quite a bit of mystery surrounding it creating both fear and intrigue, by which Satan entraps and keeps people under his control. But when the light of God shines on it and exposes the truth, much of the mystery and intrigue disappears and the true vile nature of occultism becomes visible. This in itself may be enough to set free many of Satan's captives, for Jesus said that, "you will know the truth, and the truth will set you free" (Jn. 8:32).

Criminals like to operate at night because the darkness conceals what is actually being done. Yet when a light shines in the darkness, the criminal is no longer able to carry on activity without being exposed. Satan's works in the occult are works of darkness, hidden and secretive. However, the light of God's truth will bring them out into the open. When the real nature of Satan's works are revealed, it will not be as easy for him to continue his activity, for it will be recognized for what it really is.

The Attraction of the Occult

What is it about the occult that people find so attractive? Why is it that so many are easily trapped by it? I think that it's because occultism by its very nature is so deceptive. It promises something good but is actually very evil. Too many don't discover this truth until it is too late. A hunter often uses bait to draw an unaware animal into a trap. The bait is usually food, and appeals to one of the animal's most basic desires—hunger. To the animal, the bait looks good and smells good, and he concludes that the food must be good for him. But what he doesn't know is that by going after that food, he enters into a hidden snare which will likely cost him his life. What he thought was good and would give him life, actually causes his death.

A fisherman, likewise, may use an attractive lure on the end of a line to entice the fish to bite. To the hungry fish, the lure looks like a fish, moves like a fish, and may actually smell like a fish, and so the hungry fish concludes that the lure must be a fish. However, when he bites on the lure, he may find that it was only an imitation plastic lure, not the real thing. Not only that, but there is a hook hidden inside that he could not see, and now by biting on the lure, he has been caught and will die.

Satan uses the occult in much the same way as the hunter uses bait or the fisherman uses a lure. Satan entices with that which is attractive and appeals to desires. These things may appear to be very good and desirable, yet they are mixed with falsehood, and underneath the attractive camouflage is a deadly trap or lethal hook that can result in demonic bondage and ultimately imperil a person's eternal destiny. Such was the case when Satan, in the guise of a serpent, enticed Eve to eat of the forbidden fruit by telling her that it would give her the knowledge of good and evil and make her like God. As a result, she enticed Adam to join her, they both ate of the fruit and sin and death entered the world (Gen. 3:1-6).

Four key areas in which Satan uses the occult to lure people into his trap have been identified by Lester Sumrall.[2] These four "lures" are power, knowledge, pleasure, and peace.

Power

One of the most appealing of Satan's occult lures is the lure of power. There are many things that affect a person's life about which they can do nothing—nature, the weather and the elements, and the actions of other people. But, having power makes them feel that they are in charge and in control of their life. And this is what Satan offers through the occult. Occult practices offer the practitioner a sense of power and control over their life and environment, over their fate, their future, their destiny. Also, the more power a person has, the more prestige and status they will have among others. This is also a great incentive to become adept in the occult. However, even though Satan has power, and though there are promises of power to those who practice the occult, that power is limited. It is minuscule in comparison to the unlimited power of the Almighty God. And those who practice occult powers come under bondage to the source of their power, Satan.

Knowledge

Isn't all knowledge good? Shouldn't we seek after knowledge wherever we can find it? That sounds reasonable enough, yet it is

[2] Lester Sumrall, *Supernatural Principalities and Powers*, (Nashville, TN: Thomas Nelson, 1983), pp. 13-20.

precisely what Adam and Eve sought, and it brought them nothing but misery, death, and separation from God. Knowledge of the unknown or secret things, knowledge of the hidden information that only an elite few insiders may know is very attractive. To possess such knowledge makes a person feel that they are something special. With that secret knowledge they can manipulate other people and circumstances to achieve their own personal ends.

Many occult practices are intended to reveal secret knowledge. The whole area of divination and fortune-telling are attempts to obtain such knowledge. Yet not all knowledge is good or beneficial, some may be evil or lead to evil. Certainly, that knowledge which is gained through occult means is not truth, but deceptive lies of Satan. There may be elements that are accurate, but the information has been twisted and distorted by falsehood to lead one away from truth. Also, not all means used to obtain knowledge are acceptable to God.

Pleasure

Pleasure is a great enticement. All people want to feel good, they want to have fun, they want to enjoy a good time. Satan exploits these desires through the occult, which often portrays itself as something wholesome, a positive way of self-expression. Yet, the occult is a perversion of all that is good and true, and there is much unwholesomeness involved in many occult practices.

Sexual immorality and sexual perversions may often play a part in the occult, in its rites and rituals. And although it offers momentary gratification and pleasure, there is never any lasting, genuine satisfaction. A person is always left unfulfilled and desiring something more, and is often willing to go to more degrading depths of immorality and depravity to obtain it.

Peace

The world can be a scary place to live at times and people are willing to do almost anything to obtain some sense of security, well-being, and peace. Through various occult practices, people try to eliminate annoyances, conflicts, and those things or people that they perceive as threats to their personal peace. Through magical means they hope to exercise control over their environment and other people. Through spiritistic techniques of yoga or other forms of occult meditation they seek an inner calm and harmony, yet in doing so subject themselves demonic influence bringing the opposite of what they seek—troubled minds and personality disorders.

The lure of the occult is often like that found at a carnival game or in gambling—the promise of something wonderful—a big, easy payoff. But the big win never comes, just enough small enticements to keep a person coming back with the hope that they're close to a big payoff. They get just enough out of it to cause them to commit themselves deeper and deeper and become more heavily entangled. And what few payoffs there are, end up to be counterfeits—cheap imitations. Personal hope is frustrated, and the person ends up in despair and hopelessness. With the occult, there are no winners, only losers. Only the occult is no game, it is a matter of life and death.

Children and Youth

Children and young people seem to be particularly easily lured to the occult. Generally speaking, they have not developed the maturity and skills needed to discern the dangers that it presents. Parents often leave children on their own to listen to whatever music they choose, to visit whatever websites or chat rooms catch their interest on the Internet, to play fantasy video games, or pick up books or magazines, many of which are flooded with magic and occult content. Children are spiritual creatures too, and the promise of access to something with real spiritual power is attractive to them. If parents don't lead them into a vital relationship with Jesus Christ, energized by the presence of the Holy Spirit, kids will look elsewhere.

Youngsters today face a tough challenge in modern society. They seek for answers to their problems in the occult and often find a place that seems to offer them security and power over otherwise uncontrollable circumstances. They are bombarded with images from movies and books (such as the Harry Potter series) and popular TV programs (such as Buffy the Vampire Slayer, Charmed, Angel, and Sabrina the Teenage Witch). These make magic seem empowering and encounters with demons seem exciting. Likewise, cartoons make magic seem harmless and fun. Fantasy video games give them superpowers and teach them how to use magic to manipulate and overcome others. There is much more going on here than simply appealing to a child's active imagination—there are real evil spiritual forces at work to distort spiritual truth and lead children down a destructive path.

Parents have a particular responsibility to be "nosey" and monitor the content of the activity their kids are engaged in. Be aware of the lyrics of their music, what they're reading, what they're watching, the games they are playing. Some of it you may simply have to ban from your house and prohibit them from participating in. But that should always be accompanied by an explanation appropriate to their age and perhaps substituting an acceptable form of entertainment in its place.

In other cases, you may want to watch a questionable TV program or movie with them, and then talk it over with them, using it as an object lesson, a means of teaching them the dangers of the occult and how it is in conflict with the Bible. Above all, your children need your active involvement and expressions of love in their lives, demonstrating the reality of Christ's love and power. This, accompanied by your prayers, will go a long way to safeguard them from occult dangers.[3]

Occult Phenomena: What Lies Behind Them?

What really is going on in the occult? How are occult phenomena to be explained? There are three possible answers to phenomena that appear to be supernatural:

1. Human knowledge and psychological power used to trick, deceive, or create an illusion.
2. Supernatural power that is from Satan.
3. Supernatural power that is from God.

Most of the alleged supernatural activity and phenomena that we may encounter are the result of the first of these three. It must be recognized that much of what professes to be psychic phenomena or supernatural power is nothing more than trickery or natural phenomena that have been misunderstood and misinterpreted. Occultism by its very nature is filled with lies, tricks, and deception—all of which are tools of Satan, though not necessarily being supernatural in themselves. Researchers into the psychic and supernatural have shown that the majority of what is passed off by occult practitioners as psychic or supernatural power is neither, but rather, cleverly designed tricks and fraud. If you know the "trick," then virtually any illusion of the occult practitioner can be duplicated.

---

[3] For a more complete discussion on protecting your children from the influence of the occult see chapter seven of the book by Chuck D. Pierce and Rebecca Wagner Sytsema, *Ridding Your Home of Spiritual Darkness*, (Colorado Springs, CO: Wagner Publications, 2000). See also chapters three and eight of the book by Cindy Jacobs, *Deliver Us From Evil*, (Ventura, CA: Regal Books, 2001).

There have been books written explaining the tricks and methods of illusion used, and exposing the fraud of many psychic and magic practitioners, even some of the most renowned and highly regarded psychics in the world.[4] So it needs to be kept in mind that many of the occult phenomena described in this book can be produced or created by trickery and have no genuine supernatural power.

That does not mean to say however, that they are harmless—they are not! The very act of seeking secret knowledge or power from a source of power outside of the Lord or by means which He has prohibited is in itself enough to bring about spiritual separation and alienation from God and undermine faith in Him—this is actually the greatest danger posed by occultism. And this is true whether the occult phenomena are genuinely supernatural or merely faked illusions. Ironically and tragically, though people seek after higher knowledge and abilities through the occult, Satan uses the occult to cloud their minds, hiding from them the truth that could liberate them and it moves them in a direction away from God.

However, there are events that happen or abilities that people exercise which, after attempts at natural and logical explanations have been exhausted, cannot be explained adequately except in terms of the supernatural. There are but two sources of supernatural power that are active in our world today. There is the supernatural power of Satan and the supernatural power of God.

Although these two powers may seem quite similar, they are actually quite different. There are limits to Satan's power. He can

---

[4] For an exposé on the tricks and fraud of occult practitioners see Danny Korem and Paul Meier, *The Fakers*, rev. ed. (Grand Rapids, MI: Baker Book House, 1981). Also see Andre Kole and Al Jansen, *Miracles or Magic* (Eugene, OR: Harvest House Publishers, 1987).

only work within certain boundaries which have been set by God. One of the primary ways in which Satan exercises his power and influence is through the occult. So in those instances where through occult practices, genuine supernatural power is at work, it is the manifestation of the activity of Satan and evil spirits. Thus, another danger with the occult is that whether or not a person experiences much in the way of actual supernatural power, following the occult which has its inspiration from Satan, brings a person directly into contact with evil spirits and subjects that person to various degrees of demonic influence and bondage.

Possible Effects of Occult Involvement

Seeing then that occult involvement is a turning away from God and that it leads one into subjection to satanic powers, it must be understood that the possible effects could not be good, but rather very serious. In his book, *Occult Bondage and Deliverance*, Dr. Kurt Koch, who has spent an entire career in counseling those who have come under demonic bondage as a result of their participation in the occult, has this to say:

> "First of all, what is the basic cause of occult subjection? Every sin connected with sorcery cuts a person off from God and turns him towards the worship of idols. And if a person begins to serve the devil, he will receive the devil's wages. Thus, when a person abandons God, he abandons himself at the same time. There are innumerable passages in the Bible declaring quite clearly that sorcery and occultism are terrible sins which are an abomination to the Lord and a forsaking of the living God. The following are but a few of these passages:

"Exodus 7:11-12, Exodus 22:18, Leviticus 19:26,31, Leviticus 20:6,27, 1 Samuel 28, Chronicles 10:13-14, Isaiah 2:6; 8:19, Jeremiah 27:9-10, Malachi 3:51, Zechariah 10:2, Acts 8:9, Acts 16:16, Acts 19:19, Galatians 5:20, 2 Timothy 3:8, Revelation 21:8, Revelation 22:15.

"Anyone who trespasses into Satan's domain by committing sins of sorcery will immediately be harassed by the powers of darkness, irrespective of whether he takes the step consciously or unconsciously. And the effects of this transgression of God's law make themselves felt in...different areas of a person's life."[5]

Explanation of Occult Practices

Because of the proliferation of occultism in our day it is nearly impossible to give an exhaustive listing of all occult practices and phenomena. Most occult practices are the same around the world, usually there are just some variations in form or name from place to place. What have been included are the more common ones and those most likely to be encountered. Most any occult practice will be a recognizable variation of one of these.

There is no attempt to stir up an unnatural desire in these practices by explaining them, but perhaps you have encountered some of them and were not aware of their occult nature. These explanations are to serve to awaken you to the different forms the occult takes and to be a warning against any further involvement in them. In addition to the three main categories of the occult (divination, magic, and spiritism), there are also some other occult-related objects and practices that should not be overlooked. We'll examine these first.

---

[5] Kurt Koch, *Occult Bondage and Deliverance* (Grand Rapids, MI: Kregel Publications, 1970), p. 33.

Superstitions

"Superstition is one of humankind's oldest religious preoccupations. It has been described as 'a form of personal magic used for coming to terms with the unknown.'"[6] Our practice of superstitions is supposed to give us security, protect us from danger, warn us, and give us success and prosperity. They are often couched in rhymes and familiar sayings such as, "knock on wood" or "step on a crack, break your mother's back."

They include such beliefs as kissing the blarney stone, throwing coins in a fountain or wishing well, wishing upon a star, high rise hotels or office buildings not having a 13th floor, a black cat crossing in front of you, breaking a mirror and having seven years of bad luck – the list could go on and on. It has long been forgotten where most of these began, but we do them customarily and without giving them much thought. Are they harmless? Not as much as they may seem, for what they express in reality is a form of idolatry and a lack of faith in God. There is no advantage to practicing them and they may lead to deeper involvement in the occult. Also, they are clearly not the means by which God blesses His people and so they should be abandoned.

Occult Literature

Many books on various forms of occultism can be found in local bookstores in the sections on religion, astrology and the occult, New Age, pop-psychology and self-help. If you were to go and browse those shelves, you would be astounded at how many books there are on the occult, many of which are geared to children. Most people are not aware of the danger these books pose. This listing is

---

[6] Russ Parker, *Battling the Occult* (Downer's Grove, IL: InterVarsity Press, 1990).

not an endorsement to obtain such books, but rather a warning that they are readily available and if you have these or similar books that you should dispose of them:

> **Cabala (Kabalah)**: this refers to a collection of ancient occultic mystical traditions developed among the Jewish people.
>
> **Necronomicon**: "it contains Sumerian rituals and curses that open the door to (spiritual) principalities. It is said that there are gates into the earth that these incantations open which will release demons."[7]
>
> **Eighth through Thirteenth Book of Moses**: a popular occult magic spell book.
>
> **Book of Toth**: "Egyptian occultic book that shares the wisdom of their gods. Tarot cards are based on this book."[8]
>
> **The Book of Changes (I Ching)**: "One of the classics of Chinese literature, collected and edited by Confucius into the Five Classics. Used in divination."[9]
>
> **The Book of Shadows**: "Sacred book of witchcraft. Also can refer to a notebook of occult magic spells and rituals kept by people involved in Satanism."[10]

New Age

The New Age movement is a loose-knit association of numerous individuals and organizations that share some common beliefs.

---

[7] Cindy Jacobs, *Deliver Us From Evil*, (Ventura, CA: Regal Books, 2001), p. 152.

[8] William Watson, *A Concise Dictionary of Cults and Religions* (Chicago, IL: Moody Press, 1991), p. 42.

[9] Ibid., p. 42.

[10] Ibid., p. 43.

These beliefs may be broadly stated as follows: there is ultimately one universal religion, though it may take many forms; there is a belief in karma and reincarnation, which provide a basic framework for self-improvement and development over many lifetimes; people can transform themselves into someone better and realize their fullest potential and the power to do this comes from the universal energy (Ch'i, prana, mana, etc.); the concept of God is pantheistic—God is in all and all is in God, God and the universe are one, He is not a personal being, but the Ultimate Unifying Principle that holds everything together; it affirms the godhood of people and that they are individual manifestations of God; a new World Teacher—a new avatar or master of the same status as Buddha or Jesus will come who will be the catalyst to bring in the new age.

Common Beliefs and Practices of the New Age Movement	
Altered States of Consciousness	"Christ-consciousness"
Ascended Masters	Eastern Religious Spiritual Disciplines
Auras	EST (Erhard Training Seminars)
Biofeedback	Pyramid Power
Centering	Silva Mind Control
Channeling	

Chart 6

There is a broad spectrum of religious beliefs and practices, many of an occult nature, within the New Age movement. Some of the more common are:

Altered States of Consciousness: "Phenomenon involving interruption or halting of one's normal patterns of conceptual thought and brought about by meditation, visualization, and chanting."[11]

Ascended Masters: "Disembodied spirits who have reached the highest level of spiritual consciousness and now guide the spiritual evolution of mankind. Sometimes referred to as 'enlightened masters.'"[12]

Auras: "colorful fields of energy radiating from a physical body. New Agers claim an aura is a manifestation of a person's higher self and they use the pattern of the aura to determine a person's emotional, physical, and spiritual condition."[13]

Biofeedback: "A method of bringing the heart rate, skin temperature, and brainwave pattern under control by mental concentration. Measurement instruments feed information back to the client. In some cases, biofeedback has been tried as a tool of creating altered states of consciousness."[14] This is a technique that uses electrical monitoring of brainwaves to bring normally unconscious involuntary bodily functions under conscious voluntary control. There seems to be no difficulty with this, however the real danger arises when this technique is extended to include altered states of consciousness and psychic experience.[15]

Centering: "relaxation exercises practiced by New Agers in preparation for meditation."[16]

Channeling: mediumistic practice of communicating with ascended masters and other departed spirits of the spirit world. Also known as trance channeling (see Spiritism).

Christ-consciousness: This is not an orthodox Christian concept, rather it is a "new age idea taken from Eastern mysticism and

---

[11] Watson, p. 19.
[12] Ibid., p. 28.
[13] Ibid., p. 33.
[14] Ibid., p. 40.
[15] Douglas R. Groothuis, *Unmasking the New Age* (Downers Grove, IL: Intervarsity Press, 1986), p. 60.
[16] Watson, p. 49.

Gnosticism that each person possesses the 'divine spark,' which we must realize or attain."[17]

Concepts and Practices from Eastern Religions: Many practices and terms which are common today and loosely related to occultism and the New Age movement come from Eastern religions, such as Buddhism and Hinduism. Most of the "Eastern" spiritual disciplines such as yoga and meditation have as their goal the merging together of the human soul and the "God-force" of the universe, of being one with God such that there is no distinction between humanity and divinity. These disciplines seek to discover the god within.

New Age Concepts and Practices Derived from Eastern Religions		
Avatar	Mantra	TM (Transcendental Meditation or Maharishi Technology
Chakras	Martial Arts	Yoga
Karma		

Chart 7

Avatar: "the general designation for a person considered to be the reincarnation of a Hindu deity in human form. Leaders of several Hindu sects claim to be avatars."[18]

Chakras: "Kundalini Yoga teaches that seven centers of psychic energy in the body store energy from the universal life force. Various exercises and meditations awaken these centers, allowing the power to rise up the

[17] Watson, p. 52.
[18] Ibid., p. 33.

spine, an event called kundalini. This power can be ma-
nipulated to promote healing. The ultimate result is enlightenment."[19]

Karma: "the law of retributive justice. One's karma
determines one's place in the successive stages of reincarnation. Karma represents the moral law of the universe
by which all must be judged."[20]

Mantra: A mantra is a sacred word or phrase in Sanskrit. It is repeated over and over in meditation to produce an altered state of consciousness. "Hindu tradition
believes that such words or syllables have supernatural
powers, often invoking a deity who is believed to embody
the sound."[21]

Martial Arts: A variety of fighting sports that have
their roots in ancient Eastern religion, including Buddhism
and Taoism. "The religious significance of the arts lies in
the harmonizing of life forces (Yin and Yang) and the ability to harness 'Ch'i,' [universal energy]. Masters in the
martial arts accomplish tremendous physical feats. The
ability to strike or kick with tremendous physical force or

Variations of the Martial Arts		
Aikido	Karate	Ta'i Chi Ch'uan
Judo	Kung Fu	Tae Kwan Do
Jujitsu	Ninjitsu	

Chart 8

---

[19] Watson, pp. 49-50.
[20] George A. Mather and Larry A. Nichols, *Dictionary of Cults, Sects, Religions, and the Occult* (Grand Rapids, MI: Zondervan, 1993), p. 172.
[21] Bob Larson, *Larson's New Book of Cults*, rev. ed. (Wheaton, IL: Tyndale House, 1989), p. 424.

to smash a pile of bricks with a single blow is attributed to 'Ch'i.'"[22]

Aikido: "is the most overtly religious of the martial arts. The name means 'the road to a union with the universal spirit.'"[23]

Judo: "is jujitsu without the killing aspects. Judo is more like wrestling."[24]

Jujitsu: is "a blend of kung fu and Japanese martial arts emphasizing knowing an opponent's vulnerable parts and how to attack them."[25]

Karate: mostly used in self-defense and sport-fighting.

Kung Fu: the original of the martial arts, dating "back to 2696 B.C. in an occultic form of divination called 'I Ching.'"[26]

Ninjitsu: "is a Japanese martial art form banned in the 1600s for its occultic powers. Practitioners, called Ninjas, are mercenary agents hired for covert operations involving espionage, sabotage, and assassination. They employ mind control, hypnosis, yoga, occult rituals, and other New Age practices."[27]

Ta'i Chi Ch'uan: this is "soft" kung fu. Practitioners "shadow box," concentrating on the body's psychic center. "The ultimate goal is to become an

---

[22] Mather and Nichols, *Dictionary of Cults, Sects, Religions, and the Occult*, p. 182.
[23] Watson, p. 148.
[24] Ibid., p. 148.
[25] Ibid., p. 148.
[26] Ibid., p. 147.
[27] Ibid., p. 148.

immortal by placing the body in harmony with nature." Slow movements are used with meditation to develop self-discipline and spiritual awareness."[28]

Tae Kwan Do: the Korean version of the martial arts.

Transcendental Meditation: a derivative of Hinduism cloaked in modern scientific terminology. Meditation is performed through the verbal or silent chant of a "mantra" personally assigned by the instructor at the initiation ceremony. This ceremony is a ritual which offers worship to Hindu gods and invokes their favor and presence. TM offers an advanced program which allegedly teaches students the ability to levitate, fly, and become invisible.

Yoga: the word and concept of yoga comes out of Hinduism and means the path followed so as to realize the god within. It involves the use of special postures and positions along with meditation to produce an altered state of consciousness, and ultimately to achieve union with god. All forms of yoga involve an occult philosophical base and assumptions, even that which is presented as a purely physical exercise. Although the beginning level appears only as a form of exercise or gymnastics, breathing and relaxation exercises, the advanced levels are concerned with a mastery of cosmic forces—the practice of spiritistic and magical phenomena.

---

[28] Watson, p. 148.

EST (Erhard Training Seminars): These seminars are a mixture of Eastern philosophy, humanistic psychology, and behavior modification techniques which teach pantheism, saying that we are gods of our own universe in complete control of all that happens to us.

Pyramid Power: "belief that pyramids force cosmic energy on whatever or whoever is placed underneath them. Claims to produce healing, prevent food spoilage, sweeten water, sharpen razor blades, etc."[29]

Silva Mind Control: Techniques of meditation and visualization intended to develop your control over your mind and thought processes. It is presented in terms of right-brain, left-brain theory, but actually draws on traditional methods of occult meditation and the development of psychic powers that can be used to control your environment, accomplish self-healing, etc.

Parapsychology

Parapsychology[30] is a pseudo-science that attempts to place many of the supernatural phenomena which are associated with the occult within a respectable scientific setting. It is a kind of secularization of magic which adapts it to a scientific and naturalistic world view. It claims that certain powers are "psychic," that is, latent natural powers of the human mind. However, there is little in the way of actual scientific evidence that can prove that it is actually

---

[29] Watson, p. 87.
[30] I think an accurate assessment of parapsychology is made by Douglas R. Groothuis when he says, "Despite the scientific respectability sometimes given to the paranormal, apart from the Lordship of Christ it is nothing other that the occultism prohibited throughout the Bible. It is the search for power in the wrong place. The shaman returns in scientific guise, still toting his bag of spiritual poison," *Unmasking the New Age*, p. 109.

mind-power and a great deal of conjecture and speculation. Parapsychology has yet to be vindicated scientifically.

ESP (extra sensory perception) or "sixth sense": The ability to know some information without or apart from the five "natural" senses.

Clairvoyance/Clairaudience/Clairsentience: Seeing, hearing, knowing "at a distance"; may occur while alert or in meditation or in a trance.

Telepathy/Mind Reading: The awareness of another persons thoughts.

Cognition: Consciousness of knowing about events past, present, or future.

Other Occult-Related Practices and Media

There are a number of other objects, practices, etc., that may not be a part of a religious or occult system, nevertheless they make use of occult techniques or propagate the use of occultism. Christians

Occult-Related Practices and Media	
Some Cartoons and Comic Books	Some Jewelry or Clothing
Mind-altering Drugs	Movies: Horror, Supernatural, Occult
Fantasy Role-playing Games	Religious Artifacts or Curios
Holy places: shrines, grottos, temples, caves, springs	Some forms of Music, e.g. Acid Rock, Punk, Heavy Metal, Rap, Gothic
Human or Animal Sacrifice	Some Video and Computer Games
Initiation Rites or Oaths	Some Internet Sites

Chart 9

should be aware of these and avoid them, for they may provide a link for demonic access to one's life:

Cartoons and Comic Books: "some...cartoon shows and comic books contain explicit occult overtones and material which is subtly influencing the impressionistic minds of...children. Satan finds a responsive, ready-made audience in young children in which to instill the idea that occult practices are acceptable, innocent, and even fun. He often desensitizes children to the dangers of the occult by casting cartoon and comic book heroes who use occult practices as a means of accomplishing good."[31]

Mind-Altering Drugs: The link between drugs and occult practices is ancient. The Greek word for sorcerer is *pharmakeus* from which we derive our modern words pharmacy and pharmacist. Sorcerers (witches) prepared and administered magical potions from herbs and other substances. Many of the drugs or potions used in the occult produce hallucinations and visions, some are even toxic poisons.

Fantasy Role-Playing Games: These are games that appeal particularly to young people and encourage them to "pretend" and take on the personalities and traits of the characters in the games. In the process, however, they are taught how to perform magic and cast spells, conjure demons, and other occult practices. There are many now available including such games as Dungeons and Dragons®, Tunnels and Trolls®, and DragonQuest®.

Holy Places: There are many places such as certain mountains, caves, grottos, shrines, or temples, that are reputed to have special supernatural powers, or to be the habitation of beings from the spirit-world. A person may go to one of these places for heal-

---

[31] From the booklet, *Christianity Versus the Occult* (Manila: Christian Equippers International, 1986), p. 27.

ing, to gain some special knowledge or wisdom, to obtain some supernatural power, or to commune with the spirits. The supernatural power attributed to these places is due to the activity of evil spirits.

Human or Animal Sacrifices: often a part of many occult and folk religious practices. Sacrifices are used in rituals to placate certain gods (demons) or to obtain power from them.

Initiation Rites and Oaths: many groups such as lodges, sororities, fraternities, and gangs require new members to undergo initiation rites, hazing, and to take oaths. Often these rites and oaths are derived from occultism, making use of occult magic and occult symbols. Though considered by many to be harmless, they may bring individuals under demonic bondage.

Jewelry or Clothing: much jewelry is made using the symbols of the occult, for example charmed crystals or the signs of the Zodiac. Such signs direct people away from the true God and point them in the direction of false gods. Also, there are garments made for specific religious purposes or that have magic symbols and are worn for power or protection.

Occult Movies: "Many popular motion pictures graphically portray or brazenly glorify occult and satanic practices (i.e., Rosemary's Baby, The Exorcist, Temple of Doom, Witch Mountain, Poltergeist, Ghostbusters, Omen, Friday the 13th, etc.). Grotesquely perverted plots...depicting bloody satanic rites, occult depravity, and even lycanthropy (the transformation of humans into animals and monsters)."[32]

Religious Artifacts: objects used in folk religions, non-Christian religions, or cults, temples, rites or rituals. Such objects, have been consecrated to various pagan deities (demons), and are not

---

[32] *Christianity Versus the Occult.*, p. 26.

harmless curios. They may form a link between the one who possesses it and the demon to which it is consecrated.

Rock Music: "Some popular forms of contemporary rock music (heavy metal, new wave, punk rock), promote either intentionally or not, satanic worship, values and practices. The lyrics and bizarre concert performances of such groups as KISS, Black Sabbath, AC/DC, Def Leppard, Twisted Sister, Venom, RATT, Judas Priest, Ozzy Ozborne, Iron Maiden, and Motly Crue openly promote counter-Christian values (perverted sexuality, drug use, violence) and satanic propaganda. The music of some groups even incorporates, consciously or innocuously, subliminal satanic messages in the form of backward-masking to subtly indoctrinate its youthful listeners."[33]

Video and Computer Games: Numerous video and computer games are available commercially and through on-line bulletin boards which make use of occult practices, graphic violence, and explicit sexuality. All games are not just "child's play."

What the Bible Says About Occultism

An important passage from the Bible that speaks about the occult is found in the Old Testament, in Deuteronomy 18:9-14. God had delivered the people of Israel from slavery in Egypt and now after forty years in the wilderness, was about to lead them over into the promised land. There they would live as His people and He alone would be their God. Yet, there were people living in the land that Israel was to possess and these people were engaged in many false religious and occult practices. And so, just before they enter the promised land, God gave them the following warning and instructions:

---

[33] *Christianity Versus the Occult*, p. 26.

"When you enter the land the LORD your God is giving you, do not learn to imitate the detestable ways of the nations there. Let no one be found among you who sacrifices his son or daughter in the fire, who practices divination or sorcery, interprets omens, engages in witchcraft, or casts spells, or who is a medium or spiritist or who consults the dead. Anyone who does these things is detestable to the LORD, and because of these detestable practices the LORD your God will drive out those nations before you. You must be blameless before the LORD your God. The nations you will dispossess listen to those who practice sorcery or divination. But as for you, the LORD your God has not permitted you to do so" (Deut. 18:9-13).

Because God is supreme and the only true God, He will not and cannot share His glory with any other so-called "gods." The people of Israel, whom He had saved and called to be His own, must give their total and exclusive allegiance to Him and no other. Occultism draws people away from the One True God to follow after false gods. And so, God tells His people that they cannot learn or adopt *any* of the occult practices which the current inhabitants of the land are doing.

God uses very strong language to make His point clear—occult practices are detestable to Him and anyone who practices these things is detestable to Him. In fact, it was because the inhabitants of the land were practicing these occult rites that God was bringing judgment upon them by driving them out of their homeland and giving it instead to Israel. Although the inhabitants of the land practiced the occult, God would not permit His people to do the same thing. It was strictly forbidden. His people were to be blameless before Him.

In this warning, God cites a comprehensive list of occult practices. All three of the main categories of the occult—fortune-telling, the casting of spells, contacting the spirits of the dead—are included. All are forbidden to God's people.

What was true then is true today. God still hates the practice of the occult. He forbids those who would follow Him to participate in it in any form. And His judgment rests upon those who practice the occult without repentance. God has taken a strict stand against the occult. His reason for this is simple—He loves us and He knows the dangers and harmful effects of the occult.

Chapter Five

Divination

What is Divination?

D ivination, more commonly know as *fortune-telling*, is where
a person seeks supernatural guidance or knowledge about their
own life or about other people apart from God or the means He has
given. God is not the source of knowledge obtained through divination, but rather evil spirits. Divination assumes that these spirit
beings have knowledge which humans do not possess and that they
will give them this information under the right circumstances.

There are many different classes of fortune-tellers, each with
their own methods and specialties. The various methods which are
used by them help them to discover the secret knowledge the inquirer wants to know. They may use a crystal ball, palm-reading,
astrology, omens, or many other means. All of these are ways
through which the spirit-world can communicate this information
to the fortune-teller. It must be stressed again that God is not the
One who communicates knowledge through fortune-tellers and

diviners, since divination is a practice He forbids, and He would not contradict His own word. No, whenever supernatural power is expressed in divination, it is the power of evil spirits.

Divination is used for a variety of purposes. Someone may want help in making a difficult decision, perhaps regarding marriage or their business or livelihood. Another person may want secret information about their neighbors or a particular rival that they may use against them or to get ahead. Someone else believes that with this knowledge, they can have a sense of control over their life and their future. And sometimes divination is used to try and find out the source or cause of a sickness or ailment.

Practices Used to Divine the Future

The following are some of the various methods employed by fortune-tellers to obtain secret knowledge.

Forms of Divination		
Aeromancy	Geomancy/ Feng Shui	Palmistry/ Palm Reading
Arithmancy	Haruspicy	Pendulum/Divining Rod/Dowsing

Astrology
   Zodiac
   Horoscope
	I Ching	Psychometry

Augury	Iridology	Rhapsodamancy
Candle Wax	Mirrormantic/ Crystal Ball	Significant Days and Dates
Capromancy/ Pyromancy	Numerology	Tea Leaf Reading

Card-laying/Tarot
Cards
	Omens
	   for good luck
	   for bad luck
	   to foretell events
	   bird calls	

Chart 10

Aeromancy: divination through observing the ripples on a still body of water.

Arithmancy: predicting a person's future by the use of special numbers associated with a person, especially numbers associated with the letters of their name and their birth date.

Astrology: originated in ancient Mesopotamia about 3000 BC. In this pseudo-science it is claimed that the position of the sun, moon, stars, and planets at the moment of a person's birth influences their life—their character and personality, abilities, and future.[1] Based on a person's date and time of birth, the astrologer makes a chart that attempts to decipher the supernatural meaning of the position of the heavenly bodies, and thus to foretell a person's future and destiny. This chart is called a **horoscope** and star signs are known as the **zodiac**. Astrology grew out of the belief that the heavenly bodies were gods and goddesses that determined the affairs of humanity and the events of history. Since astrology is based upon the influence of "heavenly deities," it is a form of idolatry (Deut. 4:19). Such consulting of the stars is clearly condemned and forbidden in Scripture (Deut. 17:2-5; 2 Ki. 23:4-5; Is. 47:13-15; Acts 7:43).

Augury: divination by observing the flight of birds.

Candle Wax: telling future events based on the configuration of candle wax dripped into a basin of water.

Capromancy/Pyromancy: reading the future in the configuration of fire and smoke from incense.

---

[1] "There are two kinds of astrologers, the mathematical and the mantic. The former base their predictions on mathematical evidence and statistics, focusing on personal traits and individual character. The second type employ a divinatory approach. This, at its most basic, involves subjectively reaching into the client's emotional state, coupled with suggestions which build on this knowledge. At the more sophisticated end of the scale is the operation of a definite spirit power which is very obviously not the Holy Spirit." Russ Parker, *Battling the Occult*, p. 39.

Cartomancy/Card-Laying/Tarot Cards: this practice attempts to predict a person's future by laying out cards and interpreting their meaning based on which cards appear and their relationship to each other.

Chiromancy/Palm Reading/Palmistry: the lines on the palm are given meaning and the palm is divided into seven mounds which correspond to the seven planets of astrology. It is claimed that from interpreting the lines, shapes and markings on the palm of the hand, a person's future can be foretold.

Geomancy (Feng Shui): a type of divination used to determine the appropriate site and architecture of houses, buildings, and graves to assure good fortune. Particularly common among Chinese religions.

Haruspicy: the study of the entrails of animals, usually sacrificial animals.

I Ching: a system of predicting the future and giving guidance developed in China (see occult literature above).

Iridology (Eye-Diagnosis): this is not the medical practice of recognizing certain illnesses that directly affect the eyes, but is "reading" the irises of the eyes, much in the same way as "reading" the lines on a person's palm, as a means of fortune-telling. It may be used to diagnose an illness unrelated to the eye, or to tell about a person's past or future.

Mirrormantic: the use of various objects such as **crystal balls**, **mirrors**, **rock crystals**, or **still water** which the fortune-teller uses to focus their concentration and tap into their "psychic" ability to "see" the future.

Numerology: "an occult numbering system that assigns specific values and meanings to numbers. Specific letters of the alphabet are also assigned numbers." Practitioners can then determine any number of things about people from them.[2]

Omens: events or objects that are interpreted to foretell coming events:[3]

Omens of good luck: ex. finding a toad stool or four leaf clover; seeing two shooting stars in one night; the saying, "See a pin and pick it up all the day you'll have good luck."

Omens of bad luck: ex. spilling salt; rocking an empty cradle to pass a funeral procession; walking underneath a ladder; breaking a mirror; a black cat crossing your path.

Omens that foretell events: ex. a dog eating grass means it will rain; a cat washing over its ears means a visitor will come; a spoon falling on the floor indicates a female visitor, a fork, a male visitor.

Bird calls: ex. a barn owl's cry means someone is going to die; the call of a cuckoo means that your wish will be fulfilled.

Pendulum/Divining Rod/Dowsing/Radiesthesia: a **pendulum, metal rod**, or **stick** held in the practitioner's hand which is claimed to act as a sort of "antenna" that picks up spiritual or psychic vibrations allowing the practitioner to diagnose a sickness in someone's body, or to locate water, oil, or lost objects.

Psychometry: here the practitioner holds an object that belongs to someone or which was last touched by someone and through it receives "vibrations" or insight about that particular person. This method is often used to find lost objects or people, to diagnose diseases, or foretell the future.

---

[2] George A. Mather & Larry A. Nichols, *Dictionary of Cults, Sects, Religions, and the Occult* (Grand Rapids, MI: Zondervan, 1993), p. 210.
[3] Much of this falls under what we may call superstition, as previously discussed.

Rhapsodamancy: future events are told or guidance is given by opening a sacred book and reading the first words chanced upon. Sometimes used unknowingly by Christians with the Bible.

Significant days and dates: it is claimed that for an individual, certain days or dates are significant for them for pursuing certain activities or avoiding others; ex. a fully stocked cupboard on New Year's Day means prosperity throughout the year; April 1ˢᵗ and Friday the 13ᵗʰ are unlucky days.

Tea Leaf Reading: predicting the future based on the shape and relationship of tea leaves in the bottom of a cup.

Is Divination God's Way?

Many people may have some understanding that divination is not right, yet they think that if they have good intentions that then it's okay. Or they may think to themselves, that even though they pray to God, they will consult the fortune-teller also just to be sure. But is divination really God's way? What does the Bible say?

As was already pointed out in the previous chapter, divination is explicitly forbidden by God to His people (Deut. 18:10). The prohibition is repeated in Leviticus 19:26, "Do not practice divination or sorcery." If God has forbidden it, then to practice divination is to disobey Him. And this disobedience is sin. Also, if God has forbidden it, then it can never be His will for anyone to consult a fortune-teller for any reason. Even if a person's intentions are good, it does not make something that is wrong acceptable to God—it is still wrong—it is still sin.

Why does God stand in opposition to divination? There are several reasons. But to begin with, we need to understand that God will never withhold something from us which is for our good. It is always His desire to bless those who know Him and follow Him from their hearts. In Deuteronomy 29:29, the Bible says, "The secret things belong to the LORD our God, but the things revealed belong to us and to our children forever, that we may follow all the words of this law." There are some things, which the Lord in His wisdom keeps to Himself for our own good. However, the things He has revealed, the treasury of knowledge and wisdom in Scripture, He has freely given to us that we may follow in His ways and enjoy His blessings in a loving relationship with Him.

Divination, however, is far removed from a personal relationship of faith with God. It uses means which operate independently of Him. Rather than asking God to show His will and way, divination seeks knowledge and wisdom from a source apart from God— from the spirit-world. This is a slap in the face of God. It says to God, in effect, "I don't trust You. I can be more sure of what the spirits tell me through the fortune-teller." Not only does divination require no faith in God, but it is actually an expression of unbelief in Him. Furthermore, by placing more trust in another source of wisdom and knowledge than in God, divination becomes an act of idolatry.

On one occasion in the Old Testament, the Lord told the people of Judah and the surrounding nations that Babylon was going to conquer them, yet their diviners and fortune-tellers were saying something different. God then warned them with these words, "So do not listen to your prophets, your diviners, your interpreters of dreams, your mediums or your sorcerers who tell you, 'You will not serve the king of Babylon.' They prophesy lies to you..." (Jer. 27:8-10).

Here is another clear reason why God stands against divination, because those who practice divination speak lies. They cannot be trusted to tell you the truth. Satan uses divination to lead unsuspecting people astray. For someone who wants to be sure, the only way is through prayer, to consult the Lord Jesus Christ, "in whom are hidden all the treasures of wisdom and knowledge" (Col 2:3).

Another reason of great concern regarding divination is that evil spirits are the supernatural source of knowledge behind it, not God. And so, by consulting demons through divination, people voluntarily submit to their power, influence, control, and possibly to severe degrees of demonic bondage.

God's Way

If divination is not God's way, then what is? In the Bible, we are taught that a person's life is in God's hands. We understand that God has a plan and purpose for each one of us that can never be fully realized apart from Him. We are urged to pray and seek the Lord and we are promised that He will reveal to us His plan and show us how we should go about fulfilling it. Also in Matthew 6:25-34, Jesus urges us not to worry or be anxious about life or what tomorrow may bring.

God, our loving, heavenly Father knows what we need and will care for us, "But seek first his kingdom and his righteousness, and all these things will be given to you as well. Therefore do not worry about tomorrow..." (Matt. 6:33-34). Jesus tells us not to seek from diviners, but to seek God—His Kingdom and righteousness, and then all the things we need, He will provide. This requires a personal relationship with God, a relationship characterized by faith and trust in Him.

In James 1:5 we are told, "If any of you lacks wisdom, he should ask God, who gives generously to all without finding fault, and it will be given to him." This is God's wonderful promise—if we ask of God, He will give to us freely. Our approach to God is through prayer in the name of Jesus Christ. No special rites are needed to compel God to give us answers. He is sovereign and we are to trust

Him to reveal to us what we need to know. Once we have sought God's will, we then submit ourselves to it. This is God's way, wherein there is no striving or anxiety, but rather His peace of mind and provision for us. Again as the apostle Paul encourages us, "Do not be anxious about anything, but in everything, by prayer and petition, with thanksgiving, present your requests to God. And the peace of God, which transcends all understanding, will guard your hearts and your minds in Christ Jesus" (Phil. 4:6-7).

Chapter Six

Magic

Magic Defined

*B*efore explaining what magic is, perhaps it would be helpful to explain what it is not. The magic we are concerned about is occult magic and this should be distinguished from magic as a form of entertainment. The magic of entertainment is based on "slight-of-hand" and illusion. There is no supernatural power involved. The entertainer performs "tricks" that fool the audience's power of perception. It is understood that although it appears real on stage, it is actually make believe and the audience is left to wonder, "How did he do that?" This is the magic of show business, and it is a basically innocent form of entertainment.

Occult magic, also known as sorcery, is quite different, however. It is the attempt to exercise control over people, nature, and one's environment through supernatural means. Michael Green explains, "Magic is the attempt to bring the spirit world under one's own knowledge and control. It is the precise opposite of religion, which seeks surrender to the divine, not control over it, and operates by faith not knowledge."[1]

The practitioners of occult magic make use of special charms, rituals, and incantations which will bring supernatural powers to their aid, enabling them to control aspects of their surroundings. Depending upon their need or desire, they can manipulate these supernatural powers either for their own good or someone else's harm. Merrill F. Unger explains further that magic is where people, "by incantations and ceremonies, actually influence and even control these spirit agents. The activity of such superphysical agents of evil produces the extrasensory phenomena of magic, that is occurrences that transcend the normal operation of physical law and the perception of humanity's five senses."[2]

Magic is Magic, No Matter the Name

Many treat magical and occultic practices as being morally or spiritually neutral, saying that it depends upon the motive of the practitioner and how magic is used. If magic is used to help people, it is good (white), and if it is used to harm people, it is evil (black). But this overlooks the fact that only that which is of God (the source of all that is good and perfect) can be considered morally and spiritually good.

Any practice which by its underlying philosophy contradicts God's commandments or which has been specifically forbidden by God, as with magic, must be considered evil, regardless of the intention of the practitioner. So although practitioners of magic would like to distinguish between white magic and black magic, the dis-

---

[1]   Michael Green, *Exposing the Prince of Darkness*, first American edition (Ann Arbor: Servant Publications, 1991), p. 118.
[2]   Unger, *Demons in the World Today*, p. 77.

tinction is an artificial one, not a real one. White magic and black magic both have their source of power apart from God.[3] The kingdom of Satan lies behind them both, and so white magic is nothing more than black magic in disguise.[4] The same evil supernatural powers are at work behind white magic as in black magic.

Many practitioners of "white magic" make use of Christian terminology, and symbols and objects associated with Christianity. For example, a psychic healer may have a Bible present in their "operating room," but they do not read it or try to follow it, but rather use it as a symbol and source of magic power. Many faith healers use the name of the trinity as a "magic formula" to be chanted aloud or written on a piece of paper and as used as a charm, yet they have no personal faith in the Lord Jesus Christ.

Someone may paint a cross over their windows or place a crucifix in their bedroom to protect them from harm and evil, yet to use even these symbols and objects in this way is to practice a form of magic, attributing to these objects inherent supernatural power. Genuine Christians speak words from the heart in prayer to the Father with personal faith in Jesus Christ, in whose name they pray. The one who practices white magic on the other hand, usurps authority and uses the name of God at their own discretion in an attempt to manipulate and control. White magic is severed from any personal faith in Jesus Christ, in God, or even in Scripture as God's

---

[3] "Magic normally falls into the categories of black or white, depending on whether the envisaged purposes and the spirits invoked are evil or good. The black magician seeks to subjugate his enemy. The white magician seeks to help his friend. But in the last analysis both types of magic stem from the same stock: both are attempts by means of hidden lore and secret ceremony to control. Both are an exercise in seeking power. And both conjure up spirits of the universe which are alien to Almighty God." Green, p. 118.

[4] Remember that evil spirits can disguise themselves and their activities to appear as angels of light (2 Cor 11:14).

holy Word. Many Christians may be practicing forms of white magic, unaware of what they are really doing—taking Christian signs and symbols and investing them with magical power, engaging in a form of idolatry. Kurt Koch, describes it this way:

"...the cunning camouflaging of magic by the use of Christian symbols and customs. On this last point, we can see here a process at work which we know already from the history of Israel. The brazen serpent (Num. 21:8) was given as a sign of deliverance for Israel, and prefigured the lifting up of Christ on the cross (Jn. 3:14). But this symbol

Magic		
Magic Practices	**Magic and Occult Healing**	**Witchcraft and Satanism**

Black Magic:
  Magic Persecution/Death Magic
  Magic Defense
	Psychic Healing:
	  Psychic Diagnosis
	  Psychic Healing
	  Psychic Surgery
		Witchcraft Practitioners:
		  Witch
		  Warlock
		  Sorcerer
		  Coven

White Magic	New Age/Eastern Healing:
	  Pranic Healing
	  Crystal Healing
	  Acupuncture
		Witchcraft Cults:
		  Wicca
		  Voodoo
		  Santeria
		  Macumba
		  Umbanda
		  Candomble

Sorcery	Hypnosis	Satanism
		  Traditional
		  Modern

Love Magic		Satanic Groups Church of Satan

Charms:
  Amulets
  Talisman
  Fetishes
  Magic Letters
  "Christian"
    charms
		Satanic Rites
		  Black Mass
		  Blood Subscription

Chart 11

was emptied of its real content. It became an idol. Hezekiah had to destroy this 'Nehushtan' because the people were committing idolatry with it. And so there are in the field of magic plenty of Christian symbols which have become a 'Nehushtan' to the New Testament Church."[5]

Magic Practices

While recognizing that the source of white magic and black magic is the same, it will still be helpful to use these classifications in defining different magic practices:

Black Magic: magic done to harm people; makes use of spells and magic actions with the invocation of Satan or evil spirits.

Magic persecution/death magic: a form of black magic closely linked with spiritism. Through enlisting the aid of evil spirits, the practitioner directs those spirits to attack another person, resulting for example in beatings by an invisible attacker, or the appearance of a creature in the form of a human or animal that can scratch, bite, or otherwise harm the victim.[6]

Magic defense: through various charms and spells to enlist the aid of spirits to counteract or to undo magic persecution.

White Magic: magic done to help people; use of magical powers and abilities in an unselfish way for the benefit of others, yet it has the same character and power source as black magic; may often make use of Christian terminology and symbols.

---

[5]   Kurt Koch, *Christian Counseling and Occultism* (Grand Rapids, MI: Kregel, 1980), p. 194.
[6]   Ibid., p. 49.

Comparison of White Magic with Christianity	
Christianity	**White Magic**
♦ No special objects or rituals are needed. Prayer is offered in faith.	♦ Special charms (including "Christian" symbols), incantations, or rituals are used and required. These things are believed to have inherent magical power.
♦ Faith (trust) in God alone.	♦ Faith is in the ritual or the one performing it.
♦ God is acknowledged as the Sovereign Lord. Prayer requests are submitted to the will of God.	♦ People are seen as sovereign. The attempt is made to manipulate, compel, or otherwise force God to act.
♦ The individual must have a personal relationship with God through faith in Jesus Christ.	♦ The practitioner may not be a professing, born-again Christian.

Chart 12

Sorcery: another term that refers to magic, particularly the casting of spells and mixing of potions.

Love magic: magic that is aimed at causing another person to fall in love with someone. It is a crude form of manipulation.

Magic Practitioners: magician, sorcerer, charmer, shaman.

Charms: an object on which a spell or special blessing has been written or enchanted. It may be worn or carried by a person, or placed in a person's vehicle, home, business or other property. It may serve a variety of purposes, depending upon the purpose it was made for and the particular spell or blessing which has been given to it including: protection against disease or dangers; to serve as a shield against ghosts, demons, or evil magic; or to bring good luck and good fortune.

Amulets: an object (usually natural, not man-made) that is worn or carried which transfers a certain quality to the owner such as strength, good luck, protection, etc.

Talisman: usually a picture, image, or figure worn or carried.

Fetishes: objects charged with magic powers that are carried about as a means of protection.

Magic Letters: this may include "chain letters" which promise good fortune to those who follow its instruction and bad luck to those who disregard it; letters to the saints or to the Holy Spirit in return for some favor; inscriptions on paper used for healing or good fortune.

"Christian" charms: (usually these are thought to be ineffective without the proper "blessing") scapulars, medals, crucifix; cross painted or nailed over doors or windows; "blessed palms" from Palm Sunday placed in the house; "holy water"; relics; statues; icons; prayer cloths.

The Origin of Magic and a Biblical Evaluation

When God created humanity in the garden of Eden, He said, "Be fruitful and increase in number; fill the earth and subdue it. Rule over the fish of the sea, the birds of the air and over every living creature that moves on the ground" (Gen. 1:28).

Humanity was the crowning glory of God's creation, uniquely created in His image. People were delegated to rule over and manage the whole earth on behalf of God in submission to His will. However, in the garden, they succumbed to the temptation of Satan to "be like God, knowing good and evil" (Gen. 3:5). In their desire for knowledge and power to be like God, they rebelled against God.

It is this very same desire and attitude of rebellion that underlies all occult practices, especially magic (1 Sam. 15:23). Through magic, people attempt to usurp the authority of God and take on

God's role, gaining supernatural knowledge and power apart from Him in order to control their own environment.[7]

As Unger explains, "Magic is another form of rebellion as man turned his allegiance from God and aligned himself with other gods. He not only worshipped them, but enlisted their help in his search for a knowledge and power that would enable him to live without God and in active opposition to Him."[8] Yet magic is entirely unnecessary for Christians who, through voluntary submission to God's will through Jesus Christ, are freely granted a share in His knowledge, power, and dominion.

Magic is humanity's attempt to exercise control over their environment by getting the spirit world to do their bidding. They seek to exalt themselves as the masters of nature and the masters of their own fate. However in doing so, they go outside the bounds set for them by God. And unwittingly, they do not become masters, but they become trapped and enslaved to the powers they sought to control, ending up in severe spiritual bondage to the kingdom of darkness.

"Premise, content, and symbolical form of magic spells stand in extreme opposition to the spirit of God's Word. Where God or Satan are made the handymen of human beings, man is playing the part of Lord, and we have a rebellion against the ordinances of Creation. Where man resorts to material objects like coffin nails, magic at full moon, Easter water, fetishes, women's hair, spittle, urine, burnt bones, animal carcasses, etc., there we have idolatry, there we have Belial and not Christ."[9]

---

[7] "Occultists have always tried to deny and escape the effects of the Fall and to have mastery over the environment themselves, even the cosmos. Rather than turn to God, they wish to become Him." Clifford Wilson & John Weldon, *Occult Shock and Psychic Forces* (San Diego: Master, 1980), p. 182.
[8] Unger, p. 80.
[9] Koch, p. 152.

In 2 Kings 21:1-9, we find the story of Manasseh, the king of Israel. The account is a tragic one of how he turned from the true God and led Israel into every kind of occultism.

"And he built altars for the hosts of heaven (idolatry and astrology) in the two courts of the house of the LORD. And he burned his son as an offering (human sacrifice for magical power), and practiced soothsaying and augury (divination), and dealt with mediums (spiritism) and with wizards (magic)" (2 Kings 21:5-6).

All of these things "were idolatrous practices—worshipping and transferring faith, hope, and the future from God to other practices."[10] The practice of occult magic clearly transgresses the first and third commandments, "you shall have no other gods," and, "you shall not misuse the name of the LORD your God."

Magic is strongly condemned in the Old Testament. Those who engage in magic are called "detestable" to the Lord (Deut. 18:12). And God's curse will come upon those who practice magic and none of their magic will be able to protect or save them from His judgment (Is. 47:9-12).

Magic is also consistently opposed in the New Testament. In the incident of Simon, the magician of Samaria (Acts 8:9-24), his magic abilities are contrasted with the genuine power of God demonstrated through Philip and the apostles Peter and John. On another occasion, in Paphos on the island of Cyprus, Paul was confronted with Elymas, a magician. His response to Elymas and his practice of magic was stern and unequivocal in its condemnation, "Then Saul,...filled with the Holy Spirit, looked straight at Elymas and said, 'You are a child of the devil and an enemy of everything that is right! You are full of all kinds of deceit and trickery'" (Acts 13:9-10).

---

[10] Hoover, pp. 22-23.

Magic and Healing:
A Biblical Perspective on Healing

Before looking at the practitioners and methods of occult healing, perhaps we should first set a biblical perspective for healing. Throughout His ministry, Jesus showed forth the Father's love with great sympathy and compassion, determined to heal and restore broken lives. And He did not do this merely as the means to an end, but for the sake of those in suffering and pain.

"Jesus went through all the towns and villages, teaching in their synagogues, preaching the Good News of the kingdom and healing every disease and sickness. When he saw the crowds, he had compassion on them, because they were harassed and helpless, like sheep without a shepherd" (Matt. 9:35-36).

We can clearly see in the life of Jesus that God desires to heal people. It appears that Jesus regarded His Father's ideal purpose for everyone to have complete health of body, mind, and spirit. And although that ideal was not always attained, it was what Jesus strove for in His earthly ministry and desires for us today. And so, to passively accept sickness as being the will of God or to consider it as His blessing, is to go against what we say we believe about the character of God as He has been revealed to us in Jesus Christ. God may not always heal in every circumstance, for there may be human barriers to the release of His healing power, or healing may for God's purposes be delayed. Nevertheless, God's healing is to be sought and in the meantime His grace will sustain.

A balanced view of God's will to heal is presented by Ken Blue when he says, "God wills the ultimate healing of all spiritual, psychological, and physical sickness. This complete healing comes to us through the atonement arising from the death and resurrection of Jesus Christ. We receive this final, comprehensive healing at our resurrection from the dead. So too, as a sign and seal of this promise, God often sends healing today. The healing of an illness and the grace to endure in hope when healing is delayed is the reality of God standing with us now."[11]

Jack Hayford has noted that God has appointed multiple avenues of delivering people from pain and healing them of their sicknesses. Any one of these, individually, or in combination with others, may be God's provision for a person suffering from injury, sickness, or disease:

1.   Through the natural recuperative processes that He placed in the human body when we were created.

2.   Through following proper rules of preventive health care in maintaining our bodies; i.e., climate, environment, habits, and diet.

3.   Through the charitable and skilled efforts of others by hospitals, doctors, and medicine. God has enabled us to learn something about how to alleviate pain and suffering, how to mend broken bodies, and how to save lives.

4.   Through the divine means of healing gifts distributed by the Holy Spirit and ministered in the name of the Lord Jesus Christ.

Any of the first three avenues of healing mentioned above may be exercised by anyone regardless of their spiritual relationship with God. But the healing gifts of the Holy Spirit may *only* operate through biblical Christian believers. Healing practiced by any non-Christian which taps into supernatural power, can have no other

---

[11] Ken Blue, *Authority To Heal* (Downers Grove, IL: Intervarsity Press, 1987), p. 69.

source than in Satan. Occult healing techniques are a counterfeit for the genuine healing gifts given by God through the power of the Holy Spirit. Even Christians who use occult techniques in healing, however innocently, are trespassing on forbidden ground and Douglas Groothuis wisely cautions:

"Whatever the efficacy of these various (New Age and Occultic healing) practices, the Christian must be careful to test the spirits to uncover unbiblical ideas (1 Jn. 4:1). Christians realize that the spiritual realm is real, but not uniformly benevolent. A host of rebellious spirits or demons can masquerade as agents of healing and health for the purpose of diverting attention from the Great Physician."[12]

Christians also need to be cautious about healing techniques that are called "scientific" or "medical." Medical doctors may use various healing techniques, but that does not mean that they are necessarily medically effective or scientific. As a matter of fact, medical doctors are increasingly using alternative healing techniques (occult, new age, folk medicine, shamanism). Simply because a doctor employs a particular method, does not mean that it scientifically sound, or ethically and morally correct.

Magic and Occult Healing Techniques

Practitioners of magical and occult healing:

Faith healers: where faith is focused on the healing practitioner rather than on God alone; "power" is often released through monetary gifts.

Psychic healers/Psychic surgeons: those who practice psychic healing techniques. Most "healers" in the Phil-

---

[12] Groothuis, *Unmasking the New Age*, p.66.

ippines, for example, have come from within the spiritual-
istic communities.

Psychic Healing: each of the following—psychic diagnosis, healing, and surgery—are aspects of "psychic healing." Though many
would claim that the healing is the result of the latent powers of the
mind (thus, "psychic"), or that the healer is just tapping into the
universal life-force of the cosmos, demons are the actual spirit-
forces behind these forms of healing. Psychic healing is not based
upon the techniques used, but depend greatly upon the mediumistic
powers of the one using them. Someone without occult powers
may use the same techniques, but without any positive result. In
contrast, with scientific medicine, treatment of a disease may be
done by *any* physician—it is not dependent upon any special powers.

Psychic Diagnosis: many various techniques of magic
and divination are used to discover the cause of an illness.
There is no use of valid medical methods. The diagnosis
may have no apparent connection with the ailment.

Psychic Healing: differing nonmedical methods are
used to cure a person of their diagnosed ailment. These
techniques are believed to infuse "psychic energy" into
the patient or realign a supposed energy imbalance in the
body that is believed to cause the sickness.

Psychic Surgery: this is the actual physical operation
on a person by means of supernatural power and without
the use of recognized medical techniques, training, or instruments. Usually the wound heals quickly without any
scar. The practitioner normally operates in a trance or under
the control of a spirit guide. There is some debate over the

genuineness of such operations and the majority of operations are fraudulent, being performed by illusion and slight-
of-hand tricks, however, enough evidence exists to suggest
that there are indeed instances of genuine, extraordinary
operations taking place. Also, even though references
might be made by the practitioner to the Christian religion, this is only a smokescreen, a deception to hide what
is really going on and make the psychic healing more acceptable to uninformed Christians.[13]

New Age/Eastern Healing Techniques: the religious philosophy that underlies many of these techniques is the idea that god is
an impersonal energy force and humankind is an intimate part of
this universal energy. This energy of life force in people is called
"Ch'i." "The 'Ch'i' flows through the body in two systems: Yang
and Yin. Yang is the male principle (the sun), Yin the female principle (the moon)."[14] When the flow of this energy in us is dis-
rupted or becomes unbalanced, we become sick and so various
treatments are given to readjust the body so the energy can flow
properly again. When this happens a person is healed.

Pranic Healing: healing with prana, the Sanskrit word
for "vital energy or life force." The ailments of the body
allegedly have corresponding manifestations in the "energy body." These manifestations are picked up as the
healer scans the body's "aura" with their hands, and the
healer is able to diagnose the ailment and replace a defi-

[13] For a further explanation of the phenomenon of psychic surgery see:
Johanna Michaelsen, *The Beautiful Side of Evil* (Eugene, OR: Harvest
House, 1982); Joe Folz, *Psychic Healers of the Philippines* (Plainfield,
NJ: Logos International, 1981); John Weldon and Zola Levitt, *Psychic
Healing* (Chicago, IL: Moody Press, 1982).
[14] Kurt Koch, *Occult ABC*, (Grand Rapids, MI: Kregel, 1981), p. 7.

ciency in *prana* (vital energy) or remove an excess of it through one of the eleven chakras (energy centers) of the body, thus bringing healing. There are many Hindu religious beliefs underlying pranic healing, including the concept of *karma*.

Crystal Therapy: "use of quartz crystals to heal or bring success. Crystals are believed to be conveyors of cosmic energy. Some New Agers sleep with them, wear them as pendants, or suspend them over their chairs or beds."[15]

Acupuncture: the history of acupuncture goes back about 5,000 years. The basic philosophical concept behind it grew out of astrology.[16] Acupuncture and its modern variations seek to unblock and redirect the so-called universal energy flow, "Ch'i," (God-force, or cosmic energy) through the insertion of needles or the use of pressure at key points on the body so as to balance healing energies—gold needles to strengthen the Yang (male principle) and silver needles to strengthen the Yin (female principle). The underlying philosophy is contrary to biblical Christianity. It is possible that this unwittingly involves demonic forces. Medical research has yet to establish their effectiveness or their relation to any known processes of healing.[17]

Hypnosis: an artificially induced state of consciousness similar to sleep in which the subconscious mind of the hypnotized person becomes subject to verbal manipulation by the practitioner

---

[15] Watson, *A Concise Dictionary of Cults and Religions.*
[16] Koch, *Occult ABC*, p. 7.
[17] Groothuis, pp. 60, 68.

regarding behavior and the control over some of the physiological processes of the body. Investigation has demonstrated that under hypnosis a person can be made to believe almost anything, memories can be altered or invented, and it may violate a person's will because the person in a hypnotic trance does not have a fully conscious, rational choice.[18]

The Dangers of Magic and Occult Healing

Magic and occult healing is risky and highly questionable at best. The diagnosis of illness is frequently inaccurate, often giving the wrong diagnosis for an ailment or even diagnosing conditions that do not exist. While occult healing may effect some "cures," the proven cure rate is much lower than claimed, and the effects of the cure are often temporary, with the symptoms soon returning. Misdiagnosis and improper treatment may actually cause the patient more harm – some people will in fact be in a worse condition after treatment. It may also delay them from getting genuine medical treatment that could help them and even save their life. Also, because occult healing draws upon the supernatural power of evil spirits, both practitioners and their patients may come under de-

---

[18] "There is a wide difference of opinion on the validity and usefulness of hypnotism...there is a great degree of association between hypnosis and occultism ...both occultic and the unprofessional use of hypnosis can have disastrous effects...we would strongly warn people to stay away from all forms of either occultic or entertaining hypnosis." Josh McDowell and Don Stewart *Handbook of Today's Religions* (San Bernardino, CA: Here's Life Publishers, 1983), pp. 201-202. A thorough analysis of hypnosis from a Christian perspective may be found in Martin and Diedre Bobgan, *Hypnosis and the Christian*, (Minneapolis, MN: Bethany House Publishers, 1984). They too, caution people of the dangers, "We can only warn that the deeper the induction, the greater the danger [for occult and demonic manifestations]; the deeper the trance, the more potential for harm," (p.31).

monic bondage and suffer spiritual, emotional, or mental disorders as a result.

Witchcraft and Satanism

Related to the whole area of magic are religious belief systems of which magic is an integral part. These belief systems include witchcraft and Satanism.

Witchcraft (Wicca)

Although the practice of witchcraft is ancient, modern witchcraft has no direct historical links and as practiced today was developed from the work of Gerald Gardner in the 1950s. The spiritual roots however, go back to ancient times and the worship of the goddess of nature or fertility (under the names of Isis, Kali, Lilith, Astarte, Artemis, and Diana) and the male horned god (often depicted by a goat's head, a satyr, Pan, or Baphomet). There are many variations of witchcraft some of which are expressed by members of today's radical feminist movement and extreme environmentalists, and those known by the names of their principle founders (Alexandrian, Gardnerian, Georgian, and so on).

There is no single unified belief system in witchcraft. Different groups have devised their own combinations of rites and rituals drawing from various aspects of occultism, nature worship, indigenous folk religions, and ancient mystery religions. The rituals are designed to help participants cultivate psychic/occult powers. These rituals make use of various forms of magic and may include deviant sexual behavior and animal or human sacrifice. Drug use is also a frequent aspect of witchcraft. Often herbs and drugs are used to mix potions. These potions may induce trances and hallucinations. Witchcraft is usually practiced in secret, though witches are becoming more open and vocal about their beliefs.

Witch: "a woman who uses sorcery, incantations, and magic to exercise supernatural control over things in the material world."[19]

Warlock: the male counterpart to a witch, though men may also be called witches.

Sorcerer: another name for a witch or practitioner of black magic.

Coven: this is the usual meeting of a group of witches. It is the rough parallel to a "church." Covens ideally operate in groups of thirteen individuals, normally six men and six women with a high priest or priestess leading. They usually meet on the full moon for gatherings called "esbats."

Voodoo (Haiti), Santeria (Cuba), Macumba, Umbanda, Candomble (South America): these witchcraft cults have their roots in the folk religions of the slaves from West Africa, and are a blend of occult magic, spiritism, and elements of Catholicism.

Satanism

Satanism is not a highly defined or well-organized institutional religion. There is a great deal of variety here among beliefs and practices. Generally speaking, there are two main kinds of Satanist groups:

Traditional Satanism: those practicing this kind of Satanism are usually independent, secretive, antireligious, and anti-god. It is associated with black magic, ritualism, and satanic-oriented witchcraft. The worship of a personal and powerful devil is central. Demon powers are called

---

[19] Lester Sumrall, *Supernatural Principalities and Powers*, (Nashville, TN: Thomas Nelson, 1983), p. 91.

upon. The rites and rituals of traditional Satanism may often include the use of mind-altering drugs, sexual perversion, animal or human sacrifice, and the drinking of blood.

Modern Satanism: this is a newer, more contemporary version of humanistic Satanism, exemplified in the "Church of Satan," founded by Anton LaVey, with its own Satanic Bible. It is not so much interested in how the occult works, but in knowing what to do to get the results one wants. The emphasis is on materialism and hedonism. Satan is seen more as a symbol than a real personal being.[20]

Black Mass: a ritual in Satanism which blasphemes God and ridicules Christian worship through a perversion of Christian worship liturgy.

Blood Subscription: the offering or consecration of a person to a god or deity, or to Satan, with the use of blood, often their own blood.

[20] McDowell and Stewart, pp. 237-238.

Chapter Seven

Spiritism

Spiritism Explained

Spiritism, also known as necromancy, is a spiritual activity based in the belief that people can contact or communicate with the dead or with other spirit beings. This is done to gain some "secret knowledge" that is not otherwise available or to obtain some supernatural power. The alleged communication with the dead is performed by a "medium" who enters a trancelike state, coming under the influence of some external force or "spirit guide." The medium then acts to pass on a message that supposedly has come from a deceased person,[1] usually a relative of the one making the inquiry.

Spiritists and spiritualists make use of different techniques to aid them in making contact with the spirit-world. Spiritism has

---

[1] It should be noted that some claim the beings which are communicating with and through them are aliens, extraterrestrial beings, or members of advanced civilizations from other planets.

been popularized in recent years by John Edwards who claims mediumistic abilities and his TV program, "Crossing Over," in which he gives readings and passes on messages allegedly from deceased relatives of people in the audience.

With all these various elements then, we see that spiritism, is not just something one does, but it is a whole religious outlook and approach to life, contrary to the Bible and Christianity. Joe Folz, who wrote an exposé on the Psychic Healers of the Philippines, carried out numerous interviews with individuals involved in this healing movement and discovered that virtually all came out of the spiritualist communities. He relates their understanding of spiritism, saying: "It became very clear the *espiritistas* all over the Philippines display the same characteristics. Every single *espiritista* that I asked agreed that reincarnation, Ouija boards, mediums, seances, and speaking with the dead were all integral parts of their religion. *Espiritistas* that were still in the movement as well as those who had left it all, without exception, agreed that these were fundamental precepts of their spiritual life."[2] As seen in this description, spiritism is steeped in occultism, with the objective of contacting and gaining information from the spirit-world.

We will now look at an explanation of various common phenomena and practices associated with spiritism.

Spiritistic Phenomena

These are events or happenings that are caused by the activity of demonic spirits.[3]

---

[2] Joe Folz, *Psychic Healers of the Philippines*, (Plainfield, NJ: Logos International, 1981), p. 181.

[3] Remember that most of these phenomena can be faked by occult practitioners to enhance their reputation. So this possibility needs to be ruled out before attributing these phenomena to evil spirits.

Spiritism		
Spiritistic Phenomena	**Spiritism Practitioners**	**Spiritistic Practices**
Apparitions	Spiriualists (*espiritistas*)	Psychic Healing and Psychic Surgery
Automatic Writing/ Drawing/Painting	Spiritists	Ouija Board/Spirit of the Glass
Ghosts/Poltergeists	Medium (channeler)	Necromancy
Levitation		Seance
"Little People" Dwarves Brownies Elves Goblins & Gnomes Leprechauns Trolls		Reincarnation Life Readings
Materialization		
Soul Travel/Astral Projection		
Speaking in a Trance		
Telekinesis		
Translocation		

Chart 13

Apparitions: this is the supposed appearance of the dead or a spirit being. This may be a human figure or a monstrous one. These are actually demonic spirits.

Automatic Writing (Drawing/Painting): this is when a person who is in a trance writes a message supposedly given or relayed by the spirit of a dead person.

Ghosts/Poltergeists: the appearance of a spirit being or the manifestation of spirit activity (such as unexplained noises, smells, movement of objects, etc.) which are usually associated with a particular place (haunting). Ghosts are commonly believed to be the spirits of the dead, however, this cannot be since God does not allow communication between the living and the dead. There are two possible explanations for this phenomenon: 1) they are the result of the activity of the mind through hallucinations or the imagination misinterpreting a natural phenomenon, or 2) they are the activity of evil spirits. Often, ghosts or poltergeists may be related to the past or present practice of some form of occultism in a particular place.

Levitation: when people or objects float in the air without any physical means of support.

Little People/Creatures: folk lore from many countries tell of these little people with special powers, often mischievous, sometimes helpful; most of the stories about them are imaginary, but may have some actual basis in demonic activity; dwarves (duwende—Philippines); brownies (Scotland); elves (Germany); goblins and gnomes (France); leprechauns (Ireland); trolls (Scandinavian countries).

Materializations: is the supposed appearance of the dead in material form from a substance called ectoplasm exuded from a cavity of the medium's body, occasionally occurring during a seance or similar ceremony.

Soul Travel/Astral Projection/Out of the Body Experiences: the ability claimed by some to be able to separate their soul from their body and to travel or project the "soul" to another location.

Speaking in a Trance: a message allegedly from the dead is spoken through the mouth of a person in a trance.

Telekinesis: the moving of objects without any physical or natural means, but by the supposed "psychic energy" of the mind.

Translocation: the ability claimed to be able to become invisible, travel to another location and reappear there, sometimes covering long distances in very little time.

Spiritism Practitioners

Spiritualists: those who profess to believe in the Bible and pass themselves off as a Christian group or organization, but are actually a false Christian cult that blends elements of Christianity with spiritism. They hold meetings that often include hymns, prayer, and a sermon, however the "sermon" is given by a spirit through a medium. Often the spirit claims to be one of the apostles, an angel, Mary, or even Jesus. Many other spiritistic practices and phenomena are also common.

Spiritists: these are people who practice spiritism, but make no profession or reference to Christianity.

Medium: this is a person who acts as a go-between for the living and the spirit-world. The medium often goes into a trance or altered state of consciousness, yielding their body and mind for another spirit to use. Another spirit may actually enter the medium and speak through them.

Spiritistic Practices

Psychic Healing and Psychic Surgery: (see: Magic and Occult Healing Techniques).

Ouija board/Spirit of the Glass: "a small game board containing numbers and letters used...to contact the souls of the departed during a seance. Participants sit at a table around the ouija board and place hands on a 'pointer.' the pointer is then moved around the board to various letters by the visiting spirits. The resulting message is the communication desired from the spirit world."[4]

Necromancy: the practice of consulting the dead or the spirit world. Another name for spiritism.

---

[4] Mather and Nichols, *Dictionary of Cults, Sects, Religions, and the Occult*, p. 217.

Seance: this is where a group of people join hands together in a circle and are led by a medium. The medium goes into a trance and is the go-between, passing messages back and forth between the living and the spirit-world.

Reincarnation: is based on the idea that the soul is eternal and after death moves from one body to another. When a person dies, their soul departs and is reborn in another form (animal or human). This is a common belief among Hindus, Buddhists, Confucianists, and has been adopted in one variation or another by many occult practitioners and those in the New Age movement. Reincarnation denies the resurrection, saving faith in Christ, the final judgment, and heaven and hell.

Life Readings: are a technique, frequently using hypnotism, which allegedly enables a person to go back and remember or re-live former lives. This is based on a belief in reincarnation. The actual source of information is either "false memories" created by the imagination or imparted by evil spirits.

A Biblical Evaluation of Spiritism

An important question we must ask is what spirits are really involved in spiritism? Although spiritists believe that they are contacting the spirits of deceased human beings, the Bible is clear that this cannot be the case. First of all, God has forbidden the communication between the living and the dead.[5] In Deuteronomy 18:11, God forbids persons to consult the dead. And Luke 16:27-31, Jesus, in relating the story of the rich man and Lazarus, states that the deceased rich man is not able to return to speak to his relatives.

---

[5] See Parker, *Battling the Occult*, pp. 68-69, for a discussion of the appearance of Samuel to King Saul and the appearance of Elijah and Moses on the mount of transfiguration, regarding biblical contact between the living and the dead.

This would suggest that the dead cannot contact and communicate with the living.

Secondly, Scripture teaches that when Christians die they go to be with the Lord. Those who are not Christians go to Hades to await the day of final judgment. This being so, they cannot communicate with those who are alive. It is reasonable that it works both ways and that the living, likewise cannot communicate with the dead.

In 2 Corinthians 11:14-15, Paul gives us a clue as to what is really happening, "...Satan himself masquerades as an angel of light. It is not surprising, then, if his servants (demonic spirits) masquerade as servants of righteousness." In spiritism, it is not the spirits of the dead who are contacted, but rather demonic spirits who are impersonating the dead in order to deceive the living. This means then, that the person who practices spiritism through whatever forms (seances, channeling, etc.) is not coming into contact with the spirits of the dead, but into direct contact and communication with demonic spirits. It should be obvious that this is extremely dangerous, yet these evil spirits are so skillful in deception that most people involved with spiritism are unaware of what is really happening.

We must also realize that if the spiritual power being contacted were truly of God that it would encourage the participants to acknowledge Jesus Christ as Lord and Savior. But this does not happen, even in those forms of spiritualism which take on the outward trappings of the Christian religion.

If spiritism were a divinely-appointed means of gaining knowledge and understanding, we would expect that there would be encouragement to practice spiritism in the Bible. But we cannot find this anywhere. On the contrary, Scripture speaks plainly and consistently against all forms of spiritism. In Leviticus 19:31, the Lord said, "Do not turn to mediums or seek out spiritists, for you will be defiled by them. I am the LORD your God." Again in Leviticus 20:6, He says, "I will set my face against the person who turns to mediums and spiritists to prostitute himself by following them, and I will cut him off from his people."

The act of consulting the dead is to be considered as "defiling" and as "spiritual prostitution." King Saul was one who unfortunately did not heed these words of the Lord. Faced with a conflict with the Philistines, he went to a woman who was a medium at Endor to seek advice from the prophet Samuel who had died (1 Sam. 28:3ff). The attitude of God towards what Saul did is clear in 1 Chronicles 10:13, "Saul died because he was unfaithful to the LORD; he did not keep the word of the LORD and even consulted a medium for guidance..." When people go to mediums to consult the dead, or seek direct contact with the spirit world to obtain wisdom or knowledge, they are rejecting God.

In contrast to the occult practices of spiritism, the way God has chosen to work in this world is through the lives of those who are submitted to Jesus Christ as their personal Savior and Lord. He indwells the believer with the Holy Spirit who equips them with power. But this power is acknowledged to come from God, it is submitted to His sovereign will, and can only be used according to His direction.

Dangers of Spiritism

Spiritism is a dangerous activity to engage in. Through the practice of spiritism, a person is coming into direct contact with demonic beings of the spirit-world, asking for their assistance and in many cases asking those spirits to come and indwell them. Clearly, spiritism opens the door wide and issues an invitation for demonic affliction and demonization. Even psychiatrists and psychologists, while perhaps not acknowledging the supernatural dimension, recognize the harmful effects of spiritistic activity on one's mind, emotional and mental stability. In prohibiting His people from participating in spiritism, God was not trying to prevent them from experiencing something good and helpful, but rather protecting them from something that could cause incalculable harm.

Part Three

*Escaping
the Occult Trap:*
Free at Last

Chapter Eight

Spiritual Deception and Spiritual Discernment

Whose Power Is It Really?

*I*n Acts 16:16-18, we find the story of a slave girl with supernatural ability in fortune-telling. Evidently, she was quite accurate and good at her trade for she had a good clientele, making a lot of money for her owners. When Paul and Silas came to Philippi on a preaching mission she followed them around for several days shouting out to everyone, "These men are servants of the Most High God!"

At first sight, there seems to be nothing wrong with her statement about Paul and his companions. It was accurate, besides Paul was getting some free publicity and likely more attention because of the girl. However, Paul was not happy about this situation, he was troubled by the girl's behavior. Finally after several days, he took action. Turning around to the girl he spoke to the spirit within her and said, "In the name of Jesus Christ, I command you to come out of her!" At that moment the spirit left her.

There are two key points I'd like to highlight about this incident: 1) the girl's supernatural ability was a counterfeit of the charisma God gives His people, and 2) Paul's discernment of the deception.

The girl had a supernatural ability to tell fortunes. This ability was not psychic in nature, coming from some heightened development of the natural powers of the mind. The text explicitly states that the girl "had a spirit by which she predicted the future." This spirit of divination is called in the Greek, "spirit of python," a type of serpent, and in Scripture this is symbolic of evil and deception, not of God. A demonic spirit was the source of this girl's fortune-telling power and when the spirit was cast out of her, she then lost the ability to tell fortunes.

This fortune-telling ability was a satanic counterfeit of the gifts of the Holy Spirit, which are sovereignly given to the people of God. It was a counterfeit of the spiritual gifts of knowing: word of knowledge, word of wisdom, and prophecy (1 Cor. 12:7-11), through which God imparts knowledge, insight, and/or revelation.[1]

The spiritual gifts which God gives to His people are for their edification and to draw them into a deeper and more intimate relationship with Himself. This girl's supernatural ability, however, did not seem to acknowledge Jesus Christ, was used for self-glorification and as a means of making money, even if it may have had a religious guise and was supposed to be able to be helpful.

Now Paul was able to recognize that this girl's fortune-telling ability was not of God, but of satanic origin. To do this he had to exercise discernment to evaluate, test, and judge the source of this

---

[1] This is not to be equated with the special revelation of God through Scripture. This is rather a forth-telling or foretelling of information, imparted by God for the needs of His people in a specific situation, and it is always consistent with and subservient to Scripture.

girl's power. Paul's discerning the source of this supernatural power prevented him and others from being deceived by a clever satanic counterfeit.

Satan is a liar and a deceiver. Through the host of demons under his command, he will exercise every power available to him and devise every trick imaginable in order to deceive and lead astray all humanity. He has had thousands of years of practice in refining his techniques and he's very good at it. And because Satan wants to see himself as a god and to be supreme, he will counterfeit the genuine works of God.

But Satan is not original. All he can do is come up with cheap imitations. Like a counterfeit wristwatch or counterfeit money, there is a clear distinction in quality between the copy and the real thing. In spite of his claims, Satan's counterfeits will not bring any lasting benefits, but on the contrary, only lead people into spiritual darkness and bondage. This is why it is so important that we are equipped with the truth. We need to learn to discern between the genuine works of God and the counterfeit works of Satan—that we may be set free from any bondage and protect ourselves and others from being deceived and led astray.

The Nature of Deception

What does it mean when we say someone has been deceived? It means that the person has been tricked into believing that something is true when it is actually false. Consider the thirsty man out in the heat of a barren desert who sees a mirage. In his mind he is convinced that a lush green oasis with plentiful water lies just ahead-but actually it is an optical illusion—the oasis is not really there. He has been deceived by the mirage.

Or consider a hologram, a type of photographic image projected by a laser. It appears to occupy a three-dimensional space. You can view the projected image from all sides. Your mind is convinced that there is a solid object occupying that space, but when the laser is turned off, the object disappears and all there is, is empty space. Your mind has been tricked by the hologram. Deception then, is when a person comes to believe that something is one way when in reality it is actually something quite different.

Our Response to Deception

When a person is deceived, do they know it? Are they aware that they have been tricked? No, of course not. If they were aware of the trick, then they wouldn't be deceived by it. But when someone has been deceived, and then is shown that they were tricked (that what they had previously believed to be true was in fact a lie), how do they respond? Although some people may welcome the exposé, what often happens is denial—the person does not want to acknowledge that what they have believed to be true is wrong. They may find it embarrassing, it might be a blow to their pride, and they may have become so attached to their previous belief, that even though it has been shown to be a lie, they don't want to accept it. This may be relatively harmless when we are considering a mere optical illusion, but when it comes to spiritual reality and supernatural power, it's another matter altogether.

In dealing with matters of the occult and the supernatural, it is very easy for us to be deceived and led astray. People have a natural curiosity in the supernatural and the realm of the paranormal. But generally speaking, it is an uncritical curiosity which leads them to be rather gullible and susceptible to deception by the Evil One.

In the course of reading this book you may discover that you or someone you know has been deceived in some way by the Master Deceiver. It may be that even innocently and unknowingly, you have been victimized and tricked by some of Satan's counterfeits, and were believing a lie. Don't be embarrassed by it. It can happen to anyone of us—remember our parents in the garden of Eden? But know this, if we will look to the authority of the Word of God and submit ourselves to it, as Jesus said, "You shall know the truth, and the truth shall set you free" (Jn. 8:32). If we find that we have been deceived, let's admit it, embrace the truth, and move on into freedom!

Requirements For Discernment

Evaluating supernatural power and events is not as straightforward as proving a mathematical equation or testing a scientific hypothesis, for we are dealing with the unseen spiritual realm. This realm cannot be effectively known or studied by scientific methods, although many have tried. It is not always easy to tell evil from good. For one thing, we may not know what is good and what is not and have to be taught. For another, evil may be disguised as good. In the end, the only way to know the truth about the spiritual realm and supernatural power is by God's revelation to us.

And so, in order to be able to accurately discern good and evil, to know how to distinguish the works of God from the works of Satan, there are two basic and indispensable requirements: 1) you must be a genuine believer in Jesus Christ, and 2) you must know the Word of God.

Requirement #1: Believer in Jesus Christ

Why is being a Christian a requirement for accurate discernment? Well, the Bible tells us that all people are spiritually dead (Eph. 2:1-2) and live under the dominion of Satan (1 Jn. 5:19). But when a person repents and consecrates their life to Jesus Christ, three marvelous things happen. First, they are made spiritually alive (Eph. 2:4-5). Second, they are delivered from the kingdom of Satan and brought into the kingdom of God. Jesus Christ, rather than Satan, becomes the true Lord of their life (Col. 1:13). And third, they are indwelt by the Holy Spirit (1 Cor. 6:19).

A non-Christian is blinded to spiritual truths by Satan, who rules over them (2 Cor. 4:4). In this condition they could hardly be able to accurately evaluate spiritual or supernatural phenomena. It is only when the light of God comes into their life (2 Cor. 4:6), and they give themselves over to Him that they are able to really comprehend the truth. Additionally, the Christian is indwelt by the Holy Spirit, whom Scripture describes as "the Spirit of Truth" (Jn. 16:13). He leads and guides the Christian into truth and exposes lies and falsehood.

He also helps the Christian to know and understand God. A person without the Holy Spirit (any non-Christian) cannot understand God or spiritual reality, because spiritual truths can only be understood by a spiritual person—one indwelt by the Holy Spirit (1 Cor. 2:12-14). And so, only a Christian is in a position to accurately discern the supernatural.

Requirement #2: Know the Word of God

Because we are dependent upon revelation in order to know the truth about the supernatural and spiritual realm, it is essential for us to know the Word of God. The Bible is God's special revelation to us. In it, He shows us Himself, He shows us about ourselves, and He tells us how we can live in a right relationship with Him.

He also tells us what is helpful and harmful; what is good and what is evil. He is the Creator and we are His creation. If we're to live in harmony with Him we have to live according to the pattern

He has set forth. To know how God works and what He approves of, we have to study and know the Bible. Likewise, if we want to guard ourselves from being led astray by Satan's tricks and deceit, we have to know what the Bible says, for in it, God clearly exposes Satan and his various tactics.

Peter gives his associate Timothy advice which we too would be wise to heed. He says that, "...evil men and impostors will go from bad to worse, deceiving and being deceived. But as for you, continue in what you have learned and have become convinced of, because you know those from whom you learned it, and how from infancy you have known the holy Scriptures, which are able to make you wise for salvation through faith in Christ Jesus" (2 Tim. 3:13-15).

We will inevitably be confronted by much deception, some springing from the evil intents of people's hearts and some inspired and orchestrated by Satan himself. To guard ourselves from being deceived it is essential to know the truth as God has revealed it in Scripture.

Supernatural Counterfeits

There are many instances in the Bible where there is an acknowledgment of supernatural counterfeits of the works of God. And we are given warning by these to be on the alert, lest we be taken in by supernatural deception. Let's look at a few of these passages:

Matthew 24:11, 24
"...and many false prophets will appear and deceive many people....For false Christs and false prophets will appear and perform great signs and miracles to deceive even the elect—if that were possible."

Jesus Himself warns here, that in the latter days (our time now until the return of Christ), many false prophets and christs will arise—religious or spiritual spokespersons who claim to be presenting the truth about God and spiritual reality, perhaps even presenting a "way" of salvation. In support of their claims they will perform miraculous signs and wonders, things that can only be achieved by supernatural power. However, in spite of their spiritual claims and their power to do miraculous works, they are not of God, Jesus says they are false wonderworkers, who will deceive, if possible, God's elect people.

Because these false religious prophets and messiahs are not sent or authorized by God, and yet do miraculous signs, their source of power likewise cannot be of God, but must be of Satan. Outwardly, they may appear religious and good, but the source of the inspiration of their teachings and the power of their "miracles" is satanic. It is not unlikely that many of these people may sincerely and genuinely think that they are right, that they are doing good, and even that they are serving God. They may not intentionally be deceiving people and leading them astray, but they themselves have been deceived and led astray by Satan.

Deuteronomy 13:1-5

"If a prophet or one who foretells by dreams, appears among you and announces to you a miraculous sign or wonder, and if the sign or wonder of which he has spoken takes place, and he says, 'Let us follow other gods: (gods you have not known) and let us worship them,' you must not listen to the words of that prophet or dreamer. The LORD your God is testing you to find out whether you love him with all your heart and with all your soul. It is the LORD

your God you must follow, and him you must revere. Keep
his commands and obey him. The prophet or dreamer must
be put to death,...You must purge the evil from among you."

False prophets are not a new phenomenon—they have been
around since humanity's earliest days, and Israel (God's people in
the Old Testament) was plagued with them throughout her history.
In Deuteronomy, the Lord spoke to Israel through His servant Moses,
warning them of false prophets that would at times be able to accurately predict future events and do miraculous signs and wonders.

But neither of these abilities are in themselves conclusive proof
or evidence that the person exercising these abilities is an appointed
spokesperson of God. The message of these prophets to whom
Moses refers, was not in line with God's revelation of Himself that
He had already made known, but was actually a message that encouraged the people to follow other gods. Here again, we find those
who are not sent by God exercising supernatural ability, the source
of which is satanic.

Why would God allow such false prophets to come in amongst
His people when they could stir up so much trouble and perhaps
lead many people astray? The Scripture clearly answers that it was
to test them—to see if they would hold to His revelation, abide by
His commands, and love Him exclusively with all their heart.

It is sobering to note the serious nature of the offense of being a
false prophet. It required the death penalty, "you must purge the
evil from among you." The proclamation of false teachings and the
working of miraculous signs by a supernatural power apart from
God (presumably by the power of the other gods [demons] they
were proclaiming) was evil in the sight of God and was so dangerous to the people that it had to be eliminated by drastic measures of
the death penalty.

Exodus 7:8-12, 20, 22

"The LORD said to Moses and Aaron, 'When Pharaoh says to you, 'Perform a miracle,' then say to Aaron, 'take your staff and throw it down before Pharaoh,' and it will become a snake.' So Moses and Aaron went to Pharaoh and did just as the LORD commanded. Aaron threw his staff down in front of Pharaoh and his officials, and it became a snake. Pharaoh then summoned wise men and sorcerers, and the Egyptian magicians also did the same things by their secret arts....Moses and Aaron did just as the LORD commanded. He raised his staff in the presence of Pharaoh and his officials and struck the water of the Nile, and all the water was changed into blood....But the Egyptian magicians did the same things by their secret arts, and Pharaoh's heart became hard; he would not listen to Moses and Aaron, just as the LORD had said."

In this passage, the nature of supernatural satanic counterfeits in contrast to God's genuine miracles is more easily seen. Moses and Aaron were God's appointed spokesmen. They were sent to represent God before Pharaoh. And so, on these different occasions, acting under the direct inspiration of God and in obedience to Him, they performed miracles before Pharaoh—Aaron's staff became a serpent, and the water of the Nile was turned into blood.

But in both instances, Pharaoh then called upon his own court wise men and sorcerers (magicians) and they were able to duplicate the miracles which Moses and Aaron had done. By all outward appearances they had done the same things and had access to the same power...or did they? The source of Moses and Aaron's power is clear—it was of God. But what about the Egyptian magicians—

what was the real source of their power? Scripture answers us revealing that they "...did the same things by their secret arts." Through occult practices, the magicians were able to imitate the miracles that Moses and Aaron did by the power of God. Their "miracles" were counterfeits, deceiving imitations of the genuine works of God, accomplished through satanic power.

2 Corinthians 11:13-15

"For such men are false apostles, deceitful workmen, masquerading as apostles of Christ. And no wonder, *for Satan himself masquerades as an angel of light.* It is not surprising, then, if his servants masquerade as servants of righteousness. Their end will be what their actions deserve" (emphasis added).

This passage gives us a key insight into ways in which Satan works to deceive people. Satan has under his control two groups of associates which assist him in his work. First, there are the demons/evil spirits, who willingly and knowingly serve him. Second, all people who are not in the kingdom of God are under the dominion of Satan and also willingly or unwillingly, knowingly or unknowingly, serve him.

Here it is revealed that both Satan and those who serve him (both demons and people) are not always what they appear to be. They often are like military spies or deep penetration agents who disguise themselves in order to infiltrate the opposing camp. Satan and demons, and people who have been brought under their control, may often masquerade as servants of God. Cloaked in a religious, spiritual, or some other socially or culturally acceptable guise, they proclaim a distorted message and may work "miracles" that counterfeit the works of God, and so they have the appearance of being of God, when in fact they are not.

Summary of Scriptural Insights

Let's summarize the main insights derived from these passages of Scripture:

♦ There are people who claim to be God's spokespersons, who exercise supernatural power, but who are not of God. Their power/ability is from Satan. They have been deceived and they are used by Satan to deceive others.

♦ Supernatural power therefore, in itself, may not be presumed as conclusive evidence that the power (or the person using it) are truly of God.

♦ Many of God's genuine miracles can be imitated/counterfeited by the supernatural power of Satan, usually operating through means of the occult.

♦ Satan and his servants (both demons and people) can disguise themselves as angels or servants of God in order to deceive humanity into believing and following them, rather than God.

♦ God views the exercise of supernatural powers apart from Him very seriously. Under Old Testament law it required the death penalty.

Outward appearances can be very misleading. We are warned repeatedly throughout Scripture of false prophets and teachers, those who would claim to speak in the name of God but would speak lies, have deceptive visions (the delusions of their own minds), and even work false signs and wonders (Jer. 14:14; Lam. 2:1; Matt. 24:24, 2 Pet. 2:1). And so, for us to uncritically accept or presume that all supernatural phenomena that are claimed to be for a good purpose are of God, is for us to be deceived and walk straight into one of Satan's most dangerous traps. There are many people who are claiming to be servants of God who are not operating out of the genuine power of God, nor are they receiving their "messages" through a means appointed by God, but rather by Satan's deceptive counterfeit. It is vitally important therefore, that we learn to discern the source of supernatural power.

Chapter Nine

Discerning the Source of the Supernatural

The Need to Evaluate the Supernatural

*H*aving looked at the nature of deception and the need for discernment, we now need to consider the criteria or standards by which we can test spiritual and supernatural phenomena to discern and determine what their true source is, whether they are of God or whether they are of Satan. Let me remind you also, that in order to apply these criteria with true understanding and accuracy, one must meet the requirements that have been previously explained, namely you must be a genuine believer in the Lord Jesus Christ and you must be a student of the Word of God.

Whenever we encounter an event or phenomenon that is alleged to be of spiritual, psychic, or supernatural origin, we are called upon to test it to discover what power is truly in operation.

The quickest and easiest way to be deceived and led astray is to make assumptions or jump to conclusions about the person involved or the event without first evaluating it. So, for any apparent unusual power, event, or miracle, there are several possible explanations that need to be considered. It may have a natural cause or it may have a supernatural cause.

Possible Causes of Alleged Supernatural Phenomena	
Natural Causes	Supernatural Causes
The cause behind the event is entirely natural, but unknown to the witnesses.	The cause behind the event is the supernatural intervention of satanic power.
The cause behind the event is the result of human intervention, but hidden and unknown to the witnesses.	The cause behind the event is the supernatural intervention of God.

Chart 14

Natural Causes

Any time we encounter something that is claimed to be of supernatural origin or power, the natural cause or explanation should always be considered first. There are two possibilities here: 1) the cause behind the supposed miracle or event may be entirely natural, but simply unknown, or 2) the cause may be the result of human intervention.

It is worth the effort to investigate to see if there is a natural cause. For example, it might be discovered that the supposed moaning of a ghost was actually the wind blowing through a crack in the house, or the dark demon in the corner of your room turned out to be nothing more than a shadow cast by the moonlight. All of us are prone to interpret such things according to our belief system.[1]

And it's very easy, given the right circumstances, for our imaginations to "create" supernatural events where none actually exist. If it has been determined that the event or miracle is not due to a natural cause, it could be that the event is due to human action. It is very possible for an apparently supernatural power or phenomenon to actually be caused by intentional, cleverly disguised trickery. For example, a table lifting during a seance might be due to a hidden device operated by the "medium," or the psychic surgeon's removal of some bloody mass from the abdomen might be no more than a clever slight-of-hand. Trickery and fraud are standard tools of the trade for occult practitioners. The more dramatic and spectacular the power that can be claimed by the practitioner, the greater their prestige, fame, and potential rewards.

Supernatural Causes

If all possible natural explanations for the event or miracle have been eliminated, then one has to consider the supernatural. And as has been stated before, there are two sources of supernatural power. There is the power of God and the power of Satan and evil spirits. Whenever a genuinely supernatural event occurs (e.g., healing, prophecy, apparition, etc.), then one of these two sources of power is responsible.

It would be a very serious mistake to assume that some event was caused by God, when it was actually Satan's power at work. It would likewise be a grave error to attribute to Satan that which is a genuine miracle of God. Therefore, we must make every effort to

---

[1] A person's belief system is defined by Dr. Cornelio Castillo as "the accumulated and still accumulating depository of a person's beliefs, standards, concepts, fears, biases, vocabulary—in short, everything they have in what they call awareness." The belief system has three major parts: 1) needs or desires—everything a person thinks they want for and from life, 2) perceptions—the way a person views the world around them, and 3) standards—the basis for all judgments that a person frequently makes as they go through life. From class notes in the course "A Christian Response to Occultism" at Asian Theological Seminary, Manila, 1991.

test and see which of these two powers is at work. God is not afraid, nor is He offended by someone who is making an honest attempt to apply His precepts to discover the truth behind supernatural events. In 1 John 4:1, the apostle encourages believers to test the spirits to see whether they are from God.

In order to test the supernatural and discern its source of power, we need to have some criteria to judge by, a standard by which we can measure what is of God and what is not. The following is a set of criteria, based upon the Word of God. These criteria can be applied to virtually any situation where it is believed that the supernatural is at work. By answering the questions, you will be able to see beyond the outward appearances and discover the true source of power behind it.

Evaluating Healings

In evaluating healings that claim to be accomplished through supernatural or divine power there are two main criteria by which to judge the healing and discern its source. You need to first ask, "who?" Who is the person who claims to have been the instrument of healing? Second, you need to ask, "how?" What method or means were employed to accomplish the healing?

Who?

Who is the person that was the instrument to effect the cure or healing? God works His power only through those who are His children. Only those who have been born-again and filled with His Holy Spirit, will He use as instruments of healing (Mk. 16:17-18; Jn. 14;12; 1 Cor. 12:9). Anyone without a personal, living faith in the Lord Jesus Christ, no matter what power they may have or other claims they may make, cannot be a divinely appointed channel for the healing power of God. This is an important area of evaluation, for Jesus said that there would be some who claimed to cast out demons and perform miracles in His name, but were not genuinely His disciples, and that He would disavow any knowledge of them (Matt. 7:22-23). So, being a true disciple of Jesus Christ is one of the most vital criteria. Therefore, we should ask:

1. Does the person who was the instrument for healing acknowledge Jesus Christ as their personal Lord and Savior?

2. Does this person affirm the Jesus of the Bible or some other Jesus? In other words, does this person affirm the biblical, orthodox truths about the person of Jesus Christ (i.e., eternal Son of God; Creator, born of the Holy Spirit and the virgin Mary and became man; came in the flesh, fully God and fully man in one person; without sin; died on the cross to atone for the sin of all; raised from the dead on the third day conquering sin, death, and Satan; salvation is by faith in Jesus Christ alone)?

3. What is the character of this person's life?

   a) Are they living a lifestyle in obedience to God's commandments? Are they living a moral and righteous life? (Eph. 5:5,9; 1 Jn. 3:7-10)

   b) Jesus said that you will know a good person by the good fruit of their life and a bad person by the bad fruit (Matt. 7:15-23). Does the fruit of this person's life (i.e., deeds, character, reputation) bear testimony to righteousness and godliness?

4. Does this person use this power in a selfish way, to achieve their own purposes, or for their own fame or reward?

5. Who does this person credit as the source of power? Is any person or spirit-being, other than Jesus Christ working through the Holy Spirit, credited as the source of power or inspiration?

How?

What methods, means, or techniques are used to effect the cure or healing? Apart from the natural methods of healings that God has provided,[2] He has appointed means by which He may sovereignly intervene and bring healing by His own supernatural power.

He has established prayer, offered in simple faith, to the Father, in the name of Jesus Christ as the primary means through which He effects divine healing. In response to such prayer, He will often, according to His own will and purpose, bring about healing (Jn. 16:23-24; Acts 4:9-10). Prayer for healing may be accompanied by the biblical act of the laying on of hands (Mk. 16:17-18; Lk. 4:40; Acts 28:8). Prayer for healing may also be accompanied by the biblical act of anointing with oil (Mk. 6:12-13; Jas. 5:13-16).

God may choose to also heal sovereignly through extraordinary means, such as when the woman was healed when she touched the hem of Jesus' garment (Matt. 9:20-22).[3] Yet in such special cases, healing comes at the initiative of God. Since some physical infirmities are caused by demonic bondage, healing may come as a born-again believer casts out the evil spirits in the name of Jesus Christ (Matt. 8:16-17; Acts 8:6-7; cf. Acts 16:18).

The following chart provides criteria to enable a person to evaluate the true source of power behind an alleged supernatural healing. In the column on the left are a list of traits, all of which should be present if the healing is genuinely of God. In the column on the right are a list of traits, of which if any are present would indicate that the healing is not of God, but likely of an ungodly source.

---

[2] See the discussion on "A Biblical Perspective on Healing," in Chapter Six.

[3] See also Acts 5:14; 19:12.

Criteria for Evaluating the Source
of an Alleged Supernatural Healing

If it is from God then:	If it is not from God then:
those involved will acknowledge God's sovereign will in bringing about the healing.	an attempt is made to demand, force, or manipulate a supernatural power to perform the healing rather than submitting the request for healing to God's sovereign will.
the faith of the person healed and the person who was the instrument of the healing will be centered upon Jesus Christ alone.	the faith of the people involved is centered upon the one performing the healing.
any prayer offered will be addressed to God through the mediation of Jesus Christ.	other persons or spirits from the spirit-world (such as "ascended masters" or others who have died, including the saints) or spirits (other than the Holy Spirit of God) may be invoked or called upon for aid and assistance.
the person who is the instrument of healing will be fully rational and self-controlled.	the person performing the healing may go into a trancelike state, or in some way come under the direction or control of another spirit in order to accomplish the healing.
only those means established by God in Scripture will be employed.	magical means and/or rituals are used.
the Lord Jesus Christ alone will be glorified and receive credit for the healing.	the person performing the healing or any other person or spirit-agent receives the credit or glory for the healing.
the person who is the instrument of healing is a born-again believer with personal faith in the Lord Jesus Christ.	the person who is the instrument of healing is not a born-again believer and does not profess a personal faith in the Lord Jesus Christ.

Chart 15

Evaluating Prophetic Messages, Visions, and Dreams
How Does God Speak Today?

Before looking at the criteria by which to judge a message that is alleged to come from a supernatural source, it would be helpful to briefly look at the ways in which God communicates to His people today. There are many ways in which God speaks to people today to reveal His will, His wisdom, and His knowledge. There are means which we could call ordinary means and those which could be classified as extraordinary means.

The Means by Which God May Speak Today	
Ordinary Means	**Extraordinary Means**
The Word of God: The Bible	An angel of the Lord
Counsel of godly people	Prophecy
The inner voice of the Lord; the witness of the indwelling Holy Spirit.	Dreams
	Visions

Chart 16

Ordinary Means

These are the most common and usual ways in which God will "speak" to us today:

1.   **The Word of God/Bible**: the Bible is God's special revelation to people. All that we will ever need to know about God and spiritual things may be discovered in the Scriptures. It is the one, divine, infallible, and authoritative standard by which all other revelation or spiritual insight may be measured (Ps 119:105; 2 Tim 3:16-17).

2.   **Counsel of godly people**: God may speak to us and teach us through the wise counsel of other mature born-again believers (Prov. 12:15; 13:10; 15:22).

3.   Hear the voice of the Lord: every genuine Christian has the ability to hear God speak to them in the still inner voice and conscience.

Extraordinary Means

God may, for His own purposes, also choose to speak to born-again believers through other means which are not so common.[4] I recognize that there are some within the Christian community who, with all sincerity, do not accept the possibility of God speaking through these extraordinary means today.

Although I respect those who hold this position, I do feel it is an unfortunate one, for it ascribes virtually all manifestations of spiritual power to Satan and his emissaries, and the Christian is left impotent. It is beyond the bounds of this book to explain the biblical and historical case for the contemporary manifestation of prophecy, miracles, other spiritual gifts, and extraordinary means. Many others have done this well, and if you find this a questionable issue, you may find it helpful to consult these.[5]

God has employed these extraordinary means in both the Old Testament and the New Testament. There is not sufficient biblical evidence to prove that God has ceased to use them. On the contrary, a strong case can be made for their continuance throughout the church age up to our present day. These extraordinary means which God may use are:

---

[4]   For a detailed discussion of these extraordinary means and other spiritual gifts see George Mallone, *Those Controversial Gifts* (Downers Grove: Intervarsity Press, 1983).

[5]   I would recommend the following books to the inquirer: Jack Deere, *Surprised by the Power of the Spirit* (Grand Rapids, MI: Zondervan, 1993); Charles H. Kraft, *Christianity with Power* (Manila: OMF Literature, 1989); and C. Peter Wagner, *The Third Wave of the Holy Spirit* (Ann Arbor, MI: Servant Publications, 1988).

1.   An Angel of the Lord: an angel is a messenger of God and in exceptional situations, God may send an angel with a special message to His people (Gen. 24:7; Matt. 1:20-21; Acts 8:26). It must be remembered that Satan and his forces may appear as "an angel of light" (2 Cor. 11:14-15), and so, any such alleged message must be tested carefully.

2.   Prophecy: is a gift that God gives to various Christians to receive and communicate by the Holy Spirit, an immediate, spontaneous message of God to His people. It is primarily forth-telling God's word, and may include an element of foretelling. Prophecy must not be confused with the preaching of a sermon, nor is prophecy to be understood as "fortune-telling" or any other occult practice related to telling the future. Also, not everyone who prophesies is a prophet. (Acts 13:1-2; 21;10-11; 1 Cor. 14:3).

3.   Dreams: are of two kinds: 1) those "in which the sleeper sees a connected series of images which correspond to events in everyday life," and 2) those which "may simply communicate a message from God, either directly or through angels"[6] (Gen. 20:3-7; 28:11-15; 40:9-17; Jdg 7:13-15). Not all dreams are given by God. In fact, most are the product of the human mind.

4.   Visions: usually occur to someone who is awake, often during the night. They may relate to the visible world or they may make the invisible world, visible (Gen. 46:2; 2 Ki. 6:17; Jer. 1:11-12; Acts 2:17; 10:9-16; 16:6-10).

These then, are the biblically authentic ways in which God has communicated with His people in the past and may continue to do so

---

[6]   Mallone, *Those Controversial Gifts*, p. 53.

today. Any other method or means that is employed cannot be considered to be of God.

Who?

In evaluating any "word" or "message" that claims a supernatural or divine origin, the first question to ask (as with supernatural healing), is "who" is the person through whom the prophecy or message came? God gives revelation of knowledge and wisdom *only* through those who have been born-again and filled with His Holy Spirit. So again, being a true disciple of Jesus Christ is essential if one is to speak a genuine message from God, and we should ask the same questions that are appear on page 155.

How?

Again, the second important question we must ask is "how?" How did the person who claimed to speak a "divine message" or some other supernatural information receive that message? What means did that person use in order to obtain that supernatural information? We have already looked at ways in which God communicates to His people today. We have also looked at occult means which some people use to obtain information supernaturally, but which are forbidden by God and are not used by Him. The question then of "how," is quite straight forward.

1. Did the person make use of any occult technique or method (divination, spiritism, or magic) in order to obtain information supernaturally or to receive a message? If the answer is yes, then the message or information is either a deceptive delusion of that person's mind, or it is inspired by Satan. In either case, the information cannot be of God or approved of Him.

2. Did the person receive the information or message, through one of the biblically authentic ways in which God communicates with us today? If the answer is yes, the message *may* be of God, or...it may be from the human spirit. The other two criteria of "who" and "what" still have to be answered to confirm it.

3. Is the message in order? Is the message announced publicly, in the presence of other mature Christian believers who can evaluate it? Does the person who gives the message willingly submit it to be judged by others? (1 Cor. 14:29-33).

When God speaks to people today, He may take the initiative entirely on His own, or He may respond to simple prayers from the hearts of His people. But He does not need for His people to use occult techniques to communicate with Him or to hear from Him, nor will He respond to such occult means.

What?

The third question that should be asked when someone claims to speak forth a supernatural message is "what?" What is the content of the message? The prophetic words or messages since the era of the apostles are qualitatively different than those of the Old Testament prophets and the New Testament apostles. They spoke with absolute divine authority and their words formed the canon of Scripture which is now closed and cannot be added to or taken away from.

The New Testament gift of prophecy, on the other hand, is speaking in human words something that God has brought to mind by the revelation of the Holy Spirit.[7] Yet it is subordinate revelation,[8] that is, it is subordinate to the special revelation of the Bible. The apostle

Paul instructed the churches to test prophetic words and revelation (1 Cor. 14:29-33). This means that any messages which claimed to have been of supernatural origin were not to be automatically accepted, but evaluated to determine whether or not God was truly speaking through them. Any "revelation" or "message" must be tested by the Bible, our only infallible and authoritative standard.

The chart on the following page provides criteria to enable a person to evaluate the true source of an alleged supernatural message. In the column on the left are a list of traits, all of which should be present if the message is genuinely of God. In the column on the right are a list of traits, of which if any are present would indicate that the message is not of God, but is likely a counterfeit from an ungodly source.

Evaluating the Supernatural: An Additional Asset

These criteria that have been discussed thus far, may be applied to most any situation where supernatural power is believed to be at

---

[7] For an excellent biblical study of New Testament prophecy see Wayne Grudem, *The Gift of Prophecy in the New Testament and Today* (Westchester, IL: Crossway Books, 1988). Also Bruce Yocum, *Prophecy* (Ann Arbor, MI: Servant Books, 1976).

[8] The term "subordinate revelation" has been coined by Dr. J. Rodman Williams who explains it as follows: "In addition to special revelation that is completed with the apostolic witness, God reveals Himself to those who are in the Christian community. This revelation is subordinate or secondary to the special revelation attested to in the Scriptures. ...Special revelation was given through the Old Testament prophets, Jesus Christ, and the early apostles. This revelation, centered in the Word made flesh, was prepared by the ancient prophets and completed by the early apostles. There is *nothing more to be added*: God's truth has been fully declared. Accordingly, what occurs in revelation within the Christian community is *not* new truth that goes beyond the special revelation (if so, it is spurious and not of God). It is only a deeper appreciation of what has already been revealed, or a disclosure of some message for the contemporary situation that adds nothing essentially to what He has before made known." Williams, Renewal Theology, Vol. 1, pp. 43-44.

Criteria for Evaluating *an Alleged Supernatural "Message"*	
If the message is from God then it will:	**If the message is not from God then it may:**
be in harmony with the Bible and will agree with the plain teaching of the Scriptures.	claim to be new or authoritative revelation, add or take away from the Bible, or contradict the Bible.
in some way lift up and exalt the Lord Jesus Christ; and will affirm the biblical Jesus.	lift up and exalt someone other than Jesus Christ or direct the hearer's faith or loyalty to someone other than Jesus Christ.
build up, encourage, or comfort the hearers; even if it is a word of correction or admonition, there will be a sense of the love of God reaching out to His people.	produce fear, despair, confusion, or condemnation in those who hear it.
be fulfilled and come to pass, if it has a predictive element.	make *unconditional* predictions of such things as accidents, disasters, or death.
have a witness by the Spirit of God to your spirit, that the message is true.	make predictions of the future containing *unconditional* details of specific dates or times.
willingly be submitted to be judged by the body of Christ and its leadership (1 Cor. 14:29).	give personal advice of a non-spiritual nature.
	give personal advice in contradiction to the teachings of the Bible.
	reveal personal information that is unnecessary, hurtful, or malicious.

Chart 17

work. And they can provide a simple, helpful means of discerning the source of power behind any alleged supernatural event or phenomenon. I would encourage all Christians to learn how to apply them. They are, I believe, vital to the health and vitality of the Christian community. For if Christians learn to use the critical faculties of discernment, it will allow for a freer flow of the much needed manifestations and gifts of the Holy Spirit, without an inordinate fear of "charismatic" excesses or demonic deception.

In addition to these practical means of discernment, God has provided His people with another instrument to enable them to judge the spirit behind the supernatural. It is one of many gifts of the Holy Spirit. It is called the "discerning of spirits" (1 Cor. 12:10). The word "discerning" means seeing clearly, having insight, having the power of perception. This gift, operating by the illumination of the Holy Spirit of God, enables a Christian to perceive in a particular situation what "spirit" or "spirits" are at work—whether the spiritual force behind a manifestation of power, or a person, or a message, or a situation, are motivated by the Holy Spirit, an angelic messenger, the human spirit, or demonic spirits. It enables a person to be able to distinguish the motivating spirit behind someone's words and deeds. By it, they can judge or "discern" the spiritual forces which produce certain actions, a teaching, or behavior. It is a gift of insight into the nature and activity of the spirit realm.

This gift of "discerning of spirits" does not refer to the use of mind-reading, extrasensory perception, spiritualism, mediums, or other psychic powers. And it does not require any occult divination techniques. Neither is it a natural ability to judge between good and evil. It is not even the mature judgment of those who by experience know the ways of God, people, and the devil. And it certainly isn't the ability to find the faults in the lives of others and judge them. Rather, it is discerning the spirit behind a spiritual manifestation.

This gift is an extremely valuable asset to the Christian community because when needed, the Holy Spirit can instantly provide the supernatural discernment to help in bringing deliverance to people bound by Satan, to expose error, and to expose people acting through satanic power. It is a gift Christians should ask for from God. And this, used in conjunction with sound judgment based on the criteria already discussed, will enable Christians to accurately discern the supernatural.

One final word—this function of evaluating the supernatural, although it should be done by all Christians, should especially be done within the community of believers where there are others to confirm the discernment. This provides an added component to balance the judgment of any one person.

Chapter Ten

A Method of Freedom from the Occult

*T*his book has primarily been concerned with exposing the ways in which Satan attempts to deceive us through means of the occult and supernatural. It should be evident by now, that occultism is in contradiction to God's Word. It breaks the first three commandments: "[1] You shall have no other gods before (or beside) me. [2] You shall not make for yourself an idol in the form of anything in heaven above or on the earth beneath or in the waters below. [3] You shall not bow down to them or worship them; for I, the LORD your God, am a jealous God, punishing the children for the sin of the fathers to the third and fourth generation of those who hate me, but showing love to a thousand generations of those who love me and keep my commandments" (Ex. 20:3-6).

And it invokes God's curse on those who participate in it. Any way you look at it, occultism is serious sin, even though people may have gotten involved with it unaware of its true nature. Occultism is also Satan's domain. He is the source of power behind all genuine psychic and occult phenomena. By participating in the occult, however innocently, one opens the door of access in their life to demonic harassment and possibly more severe forms of demonic bondage.

It is possible that you or someone you know has been victimized by Satan's deceptions through the occult and has come under some degree of bondage as a result. That can be a very sobering and frightful realization to come to, but even so, the good news is that God has not abandoned us to the dominion of darkness. The Lord Jesus has triumphed over all the powers of Satan and evil spirits and is ready to set the occult-involved person completely free, but they must participate and close the door by positive action and faith.

So then, what are the steps which we can take that will bring us into a full realization of spiritual freedom?

It should be understood from the outset, that only Jesus Christ can truly set a person free and make them whole in body, mind, and spirit. It is not by the power of sacred words, nor by any special method that a person may experience freedom, but only by a personal faith in the person of Jesus Christ and a living relationship with Him. Anyone who is not prepared to follow Jesus Christ on His terms as set forth in the Bible, cannot expect to find relief. Yet all who will call upon His name, and apply the truth of His Word to their lives, and appropriate for themselves by faith the victory which He has already won, can be assured of deliverance and wholeness in every part of their lives!

The steps which follow are designed to consciously bring the individual under the total Lordship of Jesus Christ and to enable them to appropriate and make real in their own personal experience the complete freedom which Jesus has already accomplished for them. Coming to experience this freedom however, frequently entails an intense spiritual battle. Satan and his minions are not likely to give up easily or without a fight. However, that is no reason to fear. Jesus came to set free the captives and release the oppressed. Moreover, He has delegated authority to His disciples and given us spiritual weapons to demolish enemy strongholds. Let's look at these.

Our Authority in Christ
Jesus Cast Out Demons

Throughout the ministry of Jesus, wherever He encountered people who were afflicted by demonic spirits, He would set them free. As the Lord of all, Jesus has supreme power and authority over creation—including demons. They must obey His commands.

For example, when Jesus encountered a severely demonized man in the region of the Gerasenes, with the word of His command, the demons were expelled and the man was healed and completely restored (Mk. 5:1-20). On another occasion, when a young boy was being tormented by an evil spirit, Jesus spoke to the demon, ordering it to leave the boy—it did and he was made whole (Mk. 9:14-29).

A significant part of Christ's work was to destroy the works of Satan and demons:

♦ "...The reason the Son of God appeared was to destroy the devil's work" (1 Jn. 3:8b).

♦ "When evening came, many who were demon-possessed were brought to him and he drove out the spirits with a word and healed all the sick" (Matt. 8:16).

♦   "...how God anointed Jesus of Nazareth with the Holy
    Spirit and power, and how he went around doing good
    and healing all who were under the power of the devil,
    because God was with him" (Acts 10:38).

Clearly one of the outstanding marks of the ministry of Jesus was
His ultimate authority over the spirit world and His unabashed con-
frontation of evil spirits whenever He came across them. When He
encountered people who had been demonized to any degree, He
ministered with compassion to their condition and gave no quarter
to the evil spirits who afflicted them.

Jesus' Disciples Are Given Authority Over Demons

But this authority which Jesus had, He did not keep to Himself
alone. Rather He delegated it to His disciples who would be co-
workers with Him. Jesus spoke first to the twelve, "...he gave them
power and authority to drive out all demons..." (Lk. 9:1). He then
sent out seventy-two others to minister with the same authority,
and when they returned they reported to Him, "Lord, even the demons submit to us in your name" (Lk. 10:17).

Throughout their ministry, the apostles continued to exercise
their authority to set free those who were demonized.

"The apostles performed many miraculous signs and wonders
among the people....Crowds gathered also from the towns around
Jerusalem, bringing their sick and those tormented by evil spirits
and all of them were healed" (Acts 5:12,16).

Philip, a deacon who also became an evangelist, is an example
of an average disciple who exercised power over the enemy:

"When the crowds heard Philip and saw the miraculous signs
he did, they all paid close attention to what he said. With shrieks,

evil spirits came out of many, and many paralytics and cripples were healed" (Acts 8:6,7).

Today's Disciples Share the Same Authority

Jesus' victory over Satan and the powers of darkness is sure (Col. 2:15) and those who are in Christ share in that victory. Jesus has also delegated to us the authority and power of His name in overcoming all the works of Satan and demons in our lives. It is time, then, to take our stand in the victorious power of Jesus Christ and use the authority He has given us. Satan would like to make us fearful and feel helpless against him, but the truth is, we are more than conquerors through Jesus Christ.

Our Weapons for Battle

We have not been left defenseless or ill-equipped to fight our enemy. We have powerful spiritual weapons with which to defeat the Evil One at every point. "For though we live in the world, we do not wage war as the world does. The weapons we fight with are not the weapons of the world. On the contrary, they have divine power to demolish strongholds" (2 Cor. 10:3,4).

Our authority and power, which have been delegated to us by the Lord Jesus Christ to be used in His name for the sake of His Kingdom, are able to overcome all the works of the enemy: "I have given you authority to trample on snakes and scorpions and to overcome all the power of the enemy; nothing will harm you. However, do not rejoice that the spirits submit to you, but rejoice that your names are written in heaven" (Lk. 10:19,20).

The Name of Jesus—no other name is greater than that of Jesus. It is not a magic word, but it represents all that Jesus Christ is, and those who believe in Him, He has authorized to act in His behalf, in His name.

♦ "Therefore God exalted him to the highest place and gave him the name that is above every name, that at the name of Jesus every knee should bow, in heaven and on earth and under the earth, and every tongue confess that Jesus Christ is Lord to the glory of God the Father" (Phil. 2:9-11).

♦ "And these signs will accompany those who believe: In my name they will drive out demons..." (Mk. 16:17).

♦ "...Finally Paul became so troubled that he turned around and said to the spirit, 'In the name of Jesus Christ I command you to come out of her!' At that moment the spirit left her" (Acts 16:18).

Spiritual Gifts (1 Cor. 12:7-11)—the various gifts of the spirit are often useful in spiritual warfare and in the ministry of deliverance, particularly the following:

♦ Discerning of Spirits—discerning the presence and working of demonic spirits in someone's life.

♦ Word of knowledge—insight about the person's problem, life, or family that can help you minister more effectively.

♦ Tongues (prayer language)—helpful when you're not sure how to pray, or the ministry becomes confusing or unsettling .

Spiritual Armor (Eph. 6:10-18)—We fight the battle and engage the enemy in the strength and power of the Lord, not our own. The armor is provided by God. It covers our vital and vulnerable parts to protect us from the enemy's attacks. We consciously put it on. And when we are thus clothed with God's armor, we will be able to withstand the enemy's attacks and stand up against Satan's schemes.

This is a different kind of battle we are in, a different kind of enemy. We are not fighting against people—others are not our enemies. But rather our struggle is "...against the rulers, against the authorities, against the powers of this dark world, and against the spiritual forces of evil in the heavenly realms" (Eph. 6:12).

We wage our battle against varying degrees, levels, and strengths of demonic powers. The armor is necessary so that in those times when you encounter enemy assaults, you will be able to stand your ground; so that you will not be overcome by the enemy, but you will overcome him!

Two other vital weapons are **the Word of God** (which is called the "sword of the spirit") and **prayer**. It is the Word of God that declares God's truth enabling us to discern truth from error and the genuine from the counterfeit. Anyone engaging in the ministry of deliverance should be well-versed in the Bible, particularly as it relates to the occult and spiritual warfare. And it is prayer which puts us in the right attitude of humility before God, acknowledging our complete reliance and dependence upon Him, and through which His power is released to flow to those afflicted by the demonic, bringing them into freedom.

The Ministry of Deliverance: Engaging the Enemy

Now that we have examined our authority and the spiritual weapons and equipment we have for confronting and defeating the enemy, let's see how we can go about applying these in a practical way so that those who have come under some form of demonic bondage may be set free.

These guidelines have been developed based on Scripture and out of experience. But ultimately, our dependence is not on any one method, but the direction of the Holy Spirit. So even if you do choose to adopt this pattern of ministry, remember that it is only a guide. Don't limit the Holy Spirit to a method.

A note to the occult-oppressed: If you are experiencing spiritual bondage as a result of occult involvement, I would strongly recommend that you actually pray through these "Steps to Freedom" and make the actual renunciations in the presence of other mature Christians with experience in this area. You can do this on your own if you feel there are no other options for you, but it is much better to pray with a team of people who have experience in the ministry of deliverance. They may act as witnesses as well as provide you with spiritual support and counsel as you make this break and step into freedom.

It has been our consistent experience that the most effective way to see people released from occult bondage is through team ministry. So at this point, I'll give an overview of the deliverance ministry team and then go on to the actual "Steps to Freedom."

The Deliverance Ministry Team
The team should have a clearly defined leader who is primarily responsible to conduct the ministry and give instructions. The leader should be someone trained and experienced in deliverance ministry. Other team members lend prayer support and appropriate counsel or insight to the leader. One person may be assigned to record what happens (i.e., demons, manifestations, relationships, etc.). It is important that team members have a sense of unity and agreement and are acquainted with the procedure that will be followed.

Personal Preparation for Ministry Team Members
Team members should allow time to pray and seek the Lord to clear the air and confess any known sin. You don't want any spiritual hindrances to interfere with your ministry. As you pray, con-

sciously put on the armor of God. Pray for God's protection over you, your family, and your team. Pray (and fast) in advance if possible, seeking the Lord's guidance and direction. Yield yourself to the Holy Spirit and be sensitive to His leading. We have found that it is good to refresh your mind and spirit with Scripture promises and songs of praise before entering the conflict.

Person Receiving Ministry and Their Family

This may be obvious, but I think is worth stating anyway—be sure that your presence and help is wanted by the person and their family and that you have their full cooperation. If not, the ministry you try to offer will likely encounter resistance and will not be properly valued. Try to select a place that is private, and free from interruptions and distractions. Select a time when everyone can use their full spiritual resources without fatigue or time limits. There are times when having other family members present during ministry is helpful. On other occasions, their presence may be a hindrance. That is a decision that needs to be made on a case-by-case basis.

Pre-Ministry Interview

When you encounter someone who has had occult exposure and who you or others suspect may be under some demonic bondage or control, before you jump to any conclusions, you need to evaluate. I have witnessed incidents of people trying to minister deliverance before they really knew what they were dealing with. The results were far from satisfactory, and in some cases added more confusion to the situation, and ended up doing more harm than good. So take time to interview the person seeking deliverance and, where possible, interview concerned members of their family.

The objectives of this time are to discern if there is actually demonic interference or influence, and then to pinpoint the demonic influence so that proper action can be taken to bring the person into freedom. The "Evaluation Checklist" in Appendix A is a tool to help you do this. Take notes on your observations and questions. Try to separate genuine facts and observations from mere speculation and assumptions. This will help you minister to the whole person and will make the time actually spent in ministry much more focused and effective.

Preliminary Diagnosis

Many factors come into play in arriving at the conclusion that specific evil spirits are at work. After having made your preliminary interviews and observations, pray and discuss briefly (among team members only), and try to clarify what you believe the Holy Spirit has revealed about the person's problem. It is helpful to identify any areas under the influence or control of evil spirit(s). For example:[1]

- Spirit of anger—a spirit which influences the way in which a particular person becomes angry or expresses anger.
- Spirit of lust—a spirit which influences the way in which a particular person becomes sexually aroused or pursues his/her desires.
- Spirit of fear—pertains to responses of becoming afraid and the ways in which such fear is expressed.

There's often an overlapping of several demonic activities. We need to recognize that a number of spirits can "cluster" in this manner. For example:

- A spirit of bitterness may also involve resentment, hatred, retaliation, or unforgiveness.

---

[1] Please note, these are not the proper names of evil spirits, but it is important to identify them in a manner sufficient to expel them.

♦ A spirit of rebellion may involve the presence of stubbornness and disobedience.

♦ A spirit of depression may involve discouragement, despair, hopelessness, despondency, suicide.

There may be further discernment and refinement as the ministry proceeds. This should be expected.

Ministry Time

As you begin the ministry time, the team leader should briefly summarize what has been discerned and then simply explain the procedure that will be followed. Next pray aloud for God's intervention and thank God for the fact that Jesus Christ is present in the midst of those who gather in His name. Then pray for spiritual protection of all those present. At this time it is appropriate to lead the person through the "Steps to Freedom" as outlined below.

At each step, there will be an explanation of the significance of the step, followed by a model prayer and suggestions for how to proceed. There is nothing special about these prayers that make them better than any others, but they do make an attempt to be very thorough. So it is suggested that you read these prayers (with understanding) as they are written. Each of these steps has a valid biblical basis and has been worked out in experience and "field tested."

I and others ministering in the area of deliverance, have found the principles represented in these steps to be very effective in dealing with the vast majority of instances of bondage through occultism. Of course, there are always exceptions. God is sovereign and is not dependent upon any method we have devised, no matter how biblically-based. He may choose to sovereignly deliver someone from occult bondage without following any of these procedures. Praise the Lord, for the times this happens!

On the other hand, there may occasionally be times, when these steps may not be adequate for a person to experience a full release. In such cases, it would be appropriate to seek out other mature believers or professional Christian counselors with more extensive experience in dealing with demonic bondage. In any case, know that God desires every person to experience complete release and freedom through Jesus Christ.

Taking the Steps to Freedom

The following are the steps that should be taken to be released from occult bondage and enter into the liberty provided by the Lord Jesus Christ:

Step One: Identify Any Occult Involvement

In preparation for the actual prayers of confession and renunciation, it is necessary to first identify any known areas of occult involvement in a person's life. In Appendix B, you will find a checklist that has been divided according to the main categories related to occultism that have been previously discussed. The individual seeking deliverance should read through the list carefully and honestly. They should place a checkmark in the appropriate space and then circle the objects or activities that apply specifically to them. Do not proceed to the remaining steps without having done this first. When this checklist has been completed, go on to step two.

Step Two: Confess Your Faith

Now that the areas of occult involvement have been identified, the next step is for the individual to confess their faith in Jesus Christ. If they have never committed their whole life to the Lord before, now is the time to do so. There is no freedom from Satan and occult bondage without bringing their life under the Lordship of

Jesus Christ. Even if they have done this before, have them do it again. Do it as a reaffirmation and testimony of their faith. In doing so, they are declaring that their trust is in Him alone as their Savior and that they are submitting their life entirely to Him as their Lord. Have them pray the following from their heart:

Prayer:
"Lord Jesus Christ, I believe that you died upon the cross to pay the full penalty of my sin and that you were raised from the dead for my salvation. I admit that I have sinned in my thoughts, words, and actions. I am deeply sorry. Right now, I turn away from all my wrong doing and I ask you to forgive me. With my whole heart, I give my life back to you and trust you alone to be my Savior. From this moment on, I acknowledge only you to be the Lord of my life and I will obediently serve you. Thank you, Lord. Amen."

Step Three: Make a "Truth Declaration"

Through means of the occult, Satan deceives with clever counterfeits of the words and works of the true and living God. When we have been deceived, it means that we have believed lies. But Jesus said that if we hold to His teaching, "You shall know the truth and the truth shall make you free" (Jn. 8:32). In order to counter the lies that Satan has previously sown in our minds (Jn. 8:44), it is important to fill and renew our minds with the truth (Rom. 12:2). This will give us a firm foundation on which to take our stand against all the schemes of the Evil One.

The following "Truth Declaration" is taken from the excellent book, *The Bondage Breaker*, by Neil Anderson and should be recited aloud. It would also be helpful for the individual to recite it on a daily basis in preparation for their ministry session and for several weeks after, in this way filling their mind with the thoughts of God from His Word. It would also be helpful for them to look up and read in their own Bible the specific verses cited.

Truth Declaration: [2]

"I recognize that there is only one true and living God, who exists as the Father, Son, and Holy Spirit. He is worthy of all honor, praise, and glory as the One who made all things and holds all things together" (see Ex. 20:2,3; Cols. 1:16,17).

"I recognize that Jesus Christ is the Messiah, the Word who became flesh and dwelt among us. I believe that He came to destroy the works of the devil, and that He disarmed the rulers and authorities and made a public display of them, having triumphed over them" (see Jn. 1:1, 14; Cols. 2:15; 1 Jn. 3:8).

"I believe that God demonstrated His own love for me in that while I was still a sinner, Christ died for me. I believe that He has delivered me from the domain of darkness and transferred me to His kingdom, and in Him I have redemption, the forgiveness of sins" (see Rom. 5:8; Cols. 1:13, 14).

"I believe that I am now a child of God and that I am seated with Christ in the heavenlies. I believe that I was saved by the grace of God through faith, and that it was a gift and not the result of any works on my part" (see Eph. 2:6,8,9; 1 Jn. 3:1-3).

---

[2] Taken from: *The Bondage Breaker*, © 2000 by Neil T. Anderson, published by Harvest House Publishers, Eugene, OR. Used by permission.

"I choose to be strong in the Lord and in the strength of His might. I put no confidence in the flesh, for the weapons of warfare are not of the flesh but are divinely powerful for the destruction of strongholds. I put on the whole armor of God. I resolve to stand firm in my faith and resist the evil one" (see 2 Corin. 10:4; Eph. 6:10-20; Phil. 3:3).

"I believe that apart from Christ I can do nothing, so I declare my complete dependence on Him. I choose to abide in Christ in order to bear much fruit and glorify my Father. I announce to Satan that Jesus is my Lord. I reject any and all counterfeit gifts or works of Satan in my life" (see Jn. 15:5, 8; 1 Corin. 12:3).

"I believe that the truth will set me free and that Jesus is the truth. If He sets me free, I will be free indeed. I recognize that walking in the light is the only path of true fellowship with God and man. Therefore, I stand against Satan's deception by taking every thought captive in obedience to Christ. I declare that the Bible is the only authoritative standard for truth and life" (see Jn. 8:32, 36; 14:6; 2 Corin. 10:5; 2 Tim. 3:15-17; 1 Jn. 1:3-7).

"I choose to present my body to God as a living and holy sacrifice and the members of my body as instruments of righteousness. I choose to renew my mind by the living Word of God in order that I may prove that the will of God is good, acceptable, and perfect. I put off the old self with its evil practices and put on the new self. I declare myself to be a new creation in Christ" (see Rom. 6:13; 12:1, 2; 2 Corin. 5:17; Cols. 3:9,10 NIV).

"By faith, I choose to be filled with the Spirit so that I can be guided into all truth. I choose to walk by the Spirit so that I will not carry out the desires of the flesh" (see Jn. 16:13; Gal. 5:16; Eph. 5:18).

"I renounce all selfish goals and choose the ultimate goal of love. I choose to obey the two greatest commandments: to love the Lord my God with all my heart, soul, mind, and strength and to love my neighbor as myself (see Matt. 22:37-39; 1 Tim. 1:5).

"I believe that the Lord Jesus has all authority in heaven and on earth, and that He is the head over all rulers and authorities. I am complete in Him. I believe that Satan and his demons are subject to me in Christ because I am a member of Christ's body. Therefore, I obey the command to submit to God and resist the devil, and I command Satan in the name of Jesus Christ to leave my presence" (see Matt. 28:18; Eph. 1:19-23; Cols. 2:10; Jas. 4:7).

Step Four: Confession of Sin and Renunciation

All participation in the occult or related activities is sin, a transgression of the commandments of God, and needs to be repented of. Any such sin for which a person remains unrepentant gives legal grounds upon which Satan can claim a right of access and can continue to hold a person in bondage.

In order to be completely free, one must acknowledge that their participation in the occult, whether knowingly or innocently, is sin and they must be willing to turn away from it completely and confess it before the Lord. It is important for a person to take a definite stand against those practices, lining themselves up with God's Word, by renouncing them.

Furthermore, there must be a rejection and renunciation of any psychic, occult, or any other supernatural power they may have gained through their participation in the occult. By doing these things, they remove themselves from these practices and bring themselves under the cleansing blood of Jesus Christ, thus denying Satan and his demonic cohorts any right of access to keep them under their power.

In the following prayer, you will notice that there is a blank space to fill in. When you come to this, refer back to the checklist in Step One, and have the person mention each item that they have previously checked off and circled which applies to. They should mention each item individually and specifically. After doing this, then continue on with the rest of the prayer.

Prayer:

"Almighty Father, in Jesus' name, I confess that I have sinned against You and broken Your commandments by: _____ (specifically name each item you have marked on the checklist). I reject and renounce all of these occult practices. I also reject and renounce all psychic, occult, or supernatural powers that I have ever had. Forgive me, Father God, and cleanse me from all unrighteousness that has come through them. I turn my back on these practices and powers never to return to them again. In Jesus' name. Amen."

Step Five: Break Psychic or Occult Ties from Past Generations

Our parents, grandparents, or other ancestors in previous generations may have been involved in some form of occultism or false religious practices, or even exercised some supernatural powers. It is possible in some cases for these powers to be transferred or passed on from one generation to the next. It is also possible for curses and demonization incurred by one generation, as a result of participating in the occult, to be passed on to succeeding generations. Thus, Satan may use the sins of their ancestors as the grounds for which to afflict them with some degree of demonic bondage. This is not to say that they are held responsible for any others' sins, but it does mean that the effects and consequences of a person's ancestors sin could affect their spiritual life and freedom. Therefore, in the following prayer, they break off from previous generations any spiritual ties of sin or bondage and any effects on their life.

Prayer:

"Father, I confess all activity on the part of my parents, grandparents, and any other ancestors which involved them in the occult as sin and I renounce those activities in the name of Jesus. I renounce and declare as null and void any oaths, vows, or pacts that my ancestors ever made to any false god, idol, cult, or false religion; any agreement they made with any evil spirit; and anything they may have said or done that allowed Satan to have an advantage in my life. In Jesus' name, I sever all ties and cancel out all demonic working that has been transferred to me from my ancestors and declare that Satan can never again use any of these things in my life. I acknowledge Jesus Christ alone as Lord in my life. Amen."

Step Six: Cancel the Effect of Any Curses

The way in which blessings and curses operate in our lives is not simply by chance or without reason. There are divine principles that have been established that govern both blessings and curses. All curses have a reason and cause behind them.

The Bible speaks of some curses that come from God. It is revealed in Scripture that these come as God's judgment upon the rebellious and ungodly, and upon those who fail to respond to what God says and are disobedient. Curses can also be brought upon us through our own words, the words of others in relationship with us, and through the servants of Satan. The main causes of curses as found in the Bible are:[3]

- ◆ Acknowledging and/or worshiping false gods
- ◆ All involvement with the occult
- ◆ Disrespect for parents
- ◆ All forms of oppression or injustice, especially when directed against the weak and the helpless
- ◆ All forms of illicit or unnatural sex
- ◆ Anti-Semitism
- ◆ Legalism, carnality, apostasy
- ◆ Theft or perjury
- ◆ Withholding from God money or other material resources to which He has a claim
- ◆ Words spoken by people with relational authority, such as father, mother, husband, wife, teacher, priest, or pastor
- ◆ Self-imposed curses
- ◆ Pledges or oaths that bind people to ungodly associations
- ◆ Curses that proceed from servants of Satan
- ◆ Soulish talk directed against other people
- ◆ Soulish prayers that accuse or seek to control other people

The Bible tells us that Jesus became a curse for us, releasing us from any curse and granting us blessing instead (Gal. 3:13-14).

---

[3] This listing is taken from Derek Prince, *Blessing or Curse—You Can Choose*, (Old Tappan, NJ: Chosen Books, Fleming Revell Company, 1990), pp. 166-167.

Jesus took upon Himself every evil consequence which our rebellion and disobedience caused and He exhausted every curse of God's broken Law so that we might receive every blessing as a result of His obedience.[4]

It is Jesus Christ alone who has obtained this exchange for us and it is only through trust in Him that we may appropriate this release from all curses and receive the fullness of the blessings of God in our own experience. In the following prayer, the individual applies by faith, to their own life situation the triumph of Christ over every curse and appropriates His blessings.

Prayer:

"Lord Jesus, I believe that through your death on the cross you became a curse for me, taking upon yourself every curse that could ever come upon me. And so I ask you to release me now from every curse over my life. In your name, I break all curses that have come upon me as a result of my own disobedience. I renounce and declare as null and void all oaths, vows, or pacts that I have ever made to any spirit being, false god, idol, cult, or false religion. I break every curse, incantation, pact, charm, spell, and all satanic arts, powers, or practices that have been made against me or my family. I break the power of every curse, negative agreement, negative pronouncement, negative confession, and every evil word that has come out of my mouth or has been spoken against me. Every curse upon me, I now turn over to you, Lord Jesus, and I place myself under the blood of your redeeming sacrifice. I receive my release and declare that no curse may any longer

---

[4] Prince, p. 183.

exercise any influence over my life or family. I receive in exchange every spiritual blessing in Jesus Christ with thanksgiving. Amen."

Step Seven: Exercise your Authority in Christ over Satan

Through personal sin and rebellion and through involvement with the occult and false religions, people have opened a door through which evil spirits may have gained entrance to their lives to bring them under bondage. However, at this point, they have already repented of these and confessed them to the Lord. In His mercy, they are forgiven. And no evil spirit has any legal claim or right to remain and keep them in slavery. Even so, they may remain unless we serve them an eviction notice. We must now evict these intruders and close the door. And we are able to do this because the same authority Jesus used to deliver others from the power of demonic trespassers has been delegated to us. We all have the authority to evict them in His name.

In the following prayer, the person reaffirms their stand of faith in the power and victory of Jesus Christ and using His authority, speaks directly to Satan and evil spirits. With a word of command, they actively participate in their own deliverance and order any evil spirits to release them and depart. In this way they close the door of their lives so that evil spirits are denied further access or reentry.

Prayer:
"Father, I come to you in the name of Jesus, thanking you for the authority that you have given me in Jesus Christ. You have said in your Word that, if I submit myself to you and resist the devil, he has to flee from me. You have said that when I use the name of Jesus which is above every

other name, Satan and all his demons must obey. So now, Lord, I claim the authority that you have given me.

"I hereby renounce you, Satan, and every evil and unclean spirit and your works in my life. I bind you from access to my body, soul, and mind—from every area of my life and I break your power and influence over me. I command you, Satan, and every evil spirit to release me and depart from me never to return. You may never have any place in me again. By an act of my will, I now close the door of my life to you forever. I belong to the Lord God Almighty. I have been redeemed by the precious blood of Jesus Christ, and I am a temple and dwelling place of the Holy Spirit. Every evil spirit is an intruder, you have no right of access or claim upon me any longer, so you must leave me now. This I declare by the authority of Jesus' mighty name.

"Father, I thank you that Jesus Christ came to bind up the brokenhearted and set the captives free. For whoever the Son sets free shall be free indeed. I thank you and praise you, my Lord, for setting me free! And I purpose in my heart to walk consistently in the liberty you have given me from this moment on, through Jesus Christ, my Lord. Amen."

At this time, the ministry team who has been leading the person though these steps, and has been praying with them will now take a more active role. The team who has been acting as witnesses to their confession and renunciation, can now be channels through which the Lord will minister more specifically and personally.

Drawing upon the information gained from the pre-ministry interview and the discernment given by the Holy Spirit, the ministry team leader should now directly confront any evil and demonic spirits perceived to be present in afflicting the person.

When confronting evil spirits, command them to obey you in Jesus' name. Here, you don't ask God to set the person free. Jesus has given you as a believer the authority and you command the evil spirits to depart in Jesus' name.

Bind Satan's influence, a sample prayer of command is:

Prayer:
"Satan, I bind you and forbid you to exercise your power in regards to this person in the name of the King of kings and Lord of lords, Jesus Christ the Son of God."

Bind the spirit(s) you're dealing with at the time from exercising dominion and power over the person (Mt. 12:29). Loose the person afflicted from bondage. Name or identify the specific spirit(s) and command it to leave in Jesus' name never to return again. A sample prayer of command is:

Prayer:
"In the name of the Lord and Savior, Jesus Christ of Nazareth, I command you evil spirits (or spirit of _____) to get out of this person right now. Be gone and leave this person alone, and remove all the evil seeds that you've planted in his/her life and body. In Jesus name!"

The "casting out" is repeated with similar words until you are satisfied that the spirits have left. Words reaffirming the victory of Jesus Christ and the defeat of the demons is often helpful, along with the commands for the evil spirits to depart. As further discernment comes in the midst of ministry, or there are other demonic spirits manifested, you may need to repeat these steps.

Helpful Notes on Ministering Deliverance

Demons may manifest and show themselves to scare or frighten you or to harm the person they're afflicting. Forbid them to do so in Jesus' name. Some manifestations you may encounter are: the eyes may roll back and flutter, pupil rolls back so only the white of the eye shows, eyes may operate independent of each other, or dilate; nostrils flair, lips purse/snarl, throat enlarges or body puffs up; persons may begin to exhibit and mimic animal like behavior or the pose of some god or deity; make animal noises—barking, hissing, roaring; excrete foul substances, vomit, etc.

There is no need to encourage outward physical manifestations. Also there is no need for screaming and shouting on the part of the ministry team. Demons respond to Jesus' authority, not lots of noise. However, being firm and confident in what you are doing is essential. When demons leave, they frequently go quietly and without drama. Sometimes though, there will be physical manifestations as the demon departs which may include yawning, coughing, screaming, weeping, or vomiting.

When you cast the spirit out, you don't need to try and tell it where to go, but you can and should forbid it to reenter. When commanding a demon, it is often good to remind them of their defeat by the blood of Jesus on the cross, and of the need to recognize and obey the authority of Jesus.

Deliverance ministry is not the time to close your eyes in prayer. It is important to keep your eyes open and for the person receiving deliverance to keep their eyes open. Always look them straight in the eye.

When casting out, speak directly to the demon. Demons may try to trick you, make deals with you, and beg. In such cases command their silence. Demons may also try to hide or "play possum." In this instance it is appropriate to command them to manifest so that they can be confronted directly. With a particularly obstinate demon, John Wimber once said, "Jesus, here is a demon that is standing against you and your church. You take care of it."

Some demons may be violent in their manifestations directed toward their victim or towards those who are ministering deliverance. If you find yourself in this situation, command the demons not to harm anyone. This should usually be enough. In some cases, it may be necessary to use physical restraint to prevent the person from hurting themselves or others. If physical restraint is necessary, this should be firm, but gentle, and absolutely as minimal as possible. *Violence or roughness by those ministering is never acceptable and should be avoided entirely.*

The ministry of deliverance is not always, but can at times be a lengthy process. If ministry goes on for a long time (for example 3-4 hours) or does not show much sign of having a positive effect, then it may be time to break off the ministry with the team going to seek the Lord in prayer and fasting for further discernment. Depending on the case, it is not uncommon to have more than one ministry session with the person.

Avoid saying, "Satan, get out!" because in virtually every case, it is not Satan who is directly present, but a demon who serves him.

Knowing When Deliverance Has Occurred

How do you know if the spirit(s) have left and gone out? Sometimes there are physical manifestations, either seen or felt; sometimes you may actually see a spirit leave; or you may have some discernment from the Holy Spirit that the spirit has left. One way to check is to have the person pray a prayer of confession such as the following:

Prayer:
"My name is _____ and I confess that Jesus Christ is my Lord and Savior. I believe with all my heart that Jesus Christ is the One and Only Son of God, that He died on the cross for me, He shed His blood for me, He was raised from the dead to give me salvation, and He lives and reigns forevermore."

If a spirit is still present, the person will be reluctant to hear about Jesus, much less talk about Him or pray to Him. The demons can discuss religious matters, and can even pray, but they will find it an immense struggle to try to open their mouth to confess that Jesus Christ died on the cross for them, that He shed His blood for them, and that He is their personal Lord and Savior from sin and its punishment. Even Christians, who have been praying all their Christian lives to God will find it difficult—during the deliverance session—to confess that Jesus died for them on the cross.

Usually, the person being delivered will know when a spirit or spirits have left. They may have a physical sensation, and there will always be a visible change in their demeanor and countenance, peace replacing the former turmoil.

In some cases where deliverance does not appear to come, it may be that there are idols, or occult or magical objects in the person's possession (perhaps even sacred stones, or other charms that have been swallowed); these may need to be removed and destroyed before complete deliverance will be experienced. For objects that have been ingested, pray for them to be vomited out or passed out.

Also, it is important to realize your limitations. There is nothing wrong with calling a halt to ministry if you're getting in over your head or are going beyond the limits of your understanding and portion of faith. In such cases it is the responsible thing to seek the assistance of someone more experienced than you, or refer the person to them. It may also be helpful to refer the person to a Christian psychiatrist or counselor who understands the value of the ministry of deliverance.

When the ministry team discerns that spiritual bondages have been broken and demonic spirits afflicting the person have left and the person receiving ministry has experienced a sense of release and freedom, it's time to move on to the next step.

Step Eight: Accept and Receive God's Forgiveness

Now is an appropriate time to celebrate and rejoice in what the Lord has done! This has been a life-changing time of ministry. Praise the Lord! The team should encourage the person to give thanks to the Lord and join with them in doing so.

Because of His faithful, boundless love for them, He has forgiven them and won the victory over everything that would bind them and keep them in darkness and under a curse! For one who has been under a heavy cloud of occult bondage and the darkness of demonic oppression, it may seem almost too good to be true, yet the Bible assures that it's real. Their freedom and deliverance is certain. Yet it wasn't easy or without a price. It cost the Lord everything—it cost His life upon the cross. Even so, He gave Himself freely. For the joy set before Him—the joy of bringing many sons and daughters to glory Jesus endured the cross, despising the shame of it (Heb. 12:2; 2:10). Jesus' work on the cross was complete, obtaining for us life and freedom. He shared in our "human-ity so that by his death he might destroy him who holds the power of death—that is, the devil—and free those who all their lives were held in slavery by their fear of death" (Heb. 2:14-15).

Spend a few moments in encouraging the person with this truth: you are forgiven and you are free! It's hard to begin to grasp even a small portion of what the Lord has done for you, but you need to accept it, receive it, and thank God for it!

That's the purpose of the following prayer. Through it, ask the person to respond to God from their heart. Have them add their own words of thanksgiving, gratitude, and love. Encourage them not to hold back, but to release their expression of love to the Lord. The more they express it, the more real it will become to them.

Prayer:
"Father, I thank you that you are true to your word. I accept your love for me and I receive your forgiveness. Thank you for giving me new life and freedom. Lord, I am yours—body, soul, and spirit. I submit to you as the Lord and Master of every area of my life. I dedicate myself, that by your grace, I will follow you in complete obedience. I give all praise and honor and glory to you Lord God. (Continue on in praise and thanksgiving in your own words. Express your love to the Lord from your heart)."

Step Nine: Destroy All Occult Related Objects

You have now led the individual through prayer, renouncing all sin and participation in occult and false religious practices. They have committed or recommitted their life to Jesus Christ, that He alone may be their Lord and Master. Now as an outward act of their total consecration to Him, they need to destroy all objects related to the occult and false religious practices. This action signifies that they have transferred any trust they have placed in these objects, and any value or significance they have given them, to the Lord. In a sense, by destroying them, they are giving them over to the Lord, as an offering, declaring by their action that Jesus is first in their life and that their trust and confidence is entirely in Him.

Whether they have actually believed in the sacredness or power of these objects, or have simply seen them as interesting curios and artifacts is irrelevant. These objects represent various forms of idolatry and occult and religious practices which have been forbidden by God and which in many cases have been dedicated to other gods. To continue to keep these things in their possession would be inconsistent with their total and exclusive allegiance to Jesus as Lord.

Additionally, any such objects serve as the physical and material point of contact between them and evil spirits. It is possible for these objects to continue to exercise a harmful spiritual influence upon their life. There is no benefit they can derive by holding on to these things. On the contrary, even though they have been freed by Jesus Christ, they may once again become ensnared by them if they do not destroy them.

The Scripture is clear that believers must make a complete break with the occult and false religious practices through destroying all such objects in their possession:

"This is what you are to do to them: Break down their altars, smash their sacred stones, cut down their Asherah poles, and burn their idols in the fire. For you are a people holy to the LORD your God...The images of their gods you are to burn in the fire. Do not covet the silver and gold on them, and do not take it for yourselves or you will be ensnared by it, for it is detestable to the LORD your God. Do not bring a detestable thing into your house or you like it will be set apart for destruction. Utterly abhor and detest it, for it is set apart for destruction" (Deut. 7:5-6; 25-26).

All such objects, the Lord declares, are detestable to Him. Would it be honoring and pleasing to the Lord for a believer to continue to have detestable things in their possession? Of course not. Our attitude toward all such objects should be like the Lord's— to utterly abhor and detest them. Regardless of their artistic or monetary value, believers must not desire them, but destroy them. In the New Testament, this seems to have also been the practice of the Early Church as people came to faith in Jesus Christ. During Paul's ministry in Ephesus we find that,

"Many of those who believed now came and openly confessed their evil deeds. A number who had practiced sorcery brought their scrolls together and burned them publicly. When they calculated the value of the scrolls, the total came to fifty thousand drachmas" (A drachma was a silver coin worth about a day's wages.) (Acts 19:18-19).

Idols were also likely included in their renunciation and destruction of objects, for a riot, incited by the craftsmen making idols, broke out some time after this public burning (Acts 19:23ff). It has been our practice in ministry to make an event of triumph out of the destruction of these objects. Such an event symbolizes the victory of Christ over the powers of evil and it brings a sense of finality and closure to the one who has been in occult bondage. Also the destruction of these objects demonstrates that these things have no spiritual or emotional hold on the person who once owned and used them.

The value of knowing Jesus, loving Him, serving Him, and walking with Him is far greater than the value of any objects a person gives up to be destroyed. The ministry team should join with the person to assist them in following through on taking the important step of destroying these objects:

1. Gather together all objects that belong to the person that have any relation to the occult or false religious practices. This should include, but not be limited to the following:[5]

    ♦ any books on the occult, new age, spiritism, fortune-telling, magic, witchcraft, or that are used in the practice of any false religion

    ♦ any magazines, comics, posters, music CDs, videos, DVDs, computer or video games that have an occult or magic or horror theme; any that express extreme sadistic or masochistic violence, or degrading and perverted forms of sexual immorality

    ♦ any objects used in fortune-telling such as crystal ball, Ouija board, tarot cards, and the like

    ♦ any astrological or magical charts, horoscopes

    ♦ any herbs and ingredients for mixing magical potions

    ♦ any objects used superstitiously or for magic such as charms, fetishes, or amulets; and jewelry associated with signs of the zodiac or depicting other pagan or occult symbols

    ♦ any equipment, supplies or paraphernalia, such as banners, cloths, candles, dolls, knives, clothing and costumes used in religious or occult rites and rituals (including regalia, jewelry, and other items associated with secret societies such as Freemasonry)

---

[5] See also Chuck D. Pierce and Rebecca Wagner Sytsema, *Ridding Your Home of Spiritual Darkness* (Colorado Springs, CO: Wagner Publications, 2000) pp. 20-24.

- any pictures, icons, statues, or figurines that represent any kind of deity, god, goddess, or "saint;" this may include Buddhas; Chinese, Hindu, Egyptian, Greek, Norse, Native American, or other depictions of gods; even so-called "Christian" images like the "sacred heart" or depictions of Mary as the "mother goddess" or "Queen of Heaven"

- any "folk art," curios, or cultural artifacts that may have religious significance or have been used in occult or religious rites including masks and pagan symbols, or artwork that manifest clear symbols of death and evil such as skulls, dragons, gargoyles, wizards, or evil fantasy creatures

- any "spirit houses," shrines or grottos in your yard or garden

2. Refer back to the checklist in Step One if you have any question about which items should be included. Only take those things that belong to you, do not take anything that belongs to someone else or are joint property, unless you first receive their permission.

3. Don't wait until some other time to destroy these objects. Make arrangements to destroy them immediately after having completed these prayers of confession, renunciation, and deliverance.

4. Don't be content with just removing these objects from display and hiding them somewhere else. Also, don't give them away or sell them, that would only pass their curse on to someone else. The Lord has instructed us to destroy them.

5. Once you have gathered these things together, take them and go along with your prayer partners to some outdoor

location to destroy them. You don't want to cause offense to those who may see you and not understand what you're doing, so make sure you have privacy. Begin with a couple of songs or choruses, and prayer that affirms our victory and freedom in Jesus Christ. Together, take apart, break up, and crush these objects, then gather them in a heap (including metal and stone) and burn them together. Give praise to the Lord for His deliverance. When you are finished, gather the ashes and any other remains and dispose of them.

A Special Word of Encouragement for Those with Occult Involvement

It may be that by this time there are some who, having read over the steps required to experience freedom, are struggling a bit by the demands of commitment and obedience that are necessary. Others may have no difficulty with it at all. But if you are one of those who are struggling with whether or not you can really follow through on these steps, allow me to share a few additional thoughts with you.

Perhaps you're wondering about what other people will think if you make a dramatic break such as this. We need to remember that if we choose to follow God, it means that sometimes He will require us to do things that other people are not happy about. It means that we may stand out from the crowd. And yet the Bible says, "come out from among them and be separate" (2 Cor. 6:17). And, "do you not know that friendship with the world is hostility toward God? Therefore, whoever wishes to be a friend of the world makes himself and enemy of God?" (James 4:4). We are to live in the world, but not live according to the ways of the world. If we put the Lord first and consider obedience to Him as more impor-

tant than anything else, it will definitely affect our lives, and perhaps the way others behave toward us.

It is possible that there will even be misunderstanding by those
very close to you, by members of your own family. Although you
should do everything possible to eliminate those misunderstand-
ings and to honor your family, as a Christian your first loyalty belongs to the Lord and obedience to His Word. The Lord reassures
us and encourages us not to be afraid of how others may react to us
because we follow Him. He has promised to care for us and all
these other concerns He will take care of also, if we put Him first
and obey His commands (Matt. 10:28-31).

In the end, we have to decide if it's more important for us to
please others and gain their approval or to please God and win His
praise. "So we make it our goal to please Him... For we must all
appear before the judgment seat of Christ, that each one may receive what is due him for the things done while in the body, whether
good or bad" (2 Cor. 5:9-10).

God has clearly shown in His Word that those who are called
by His name—Christians—may not have anything to do with the
occult, idolatry, or any other false religious practices. It is also
clear that all the practices and objects related to them are detestable to Him. There is nothing that can make what God has declared unacceptable to become acceptable. There is no special
blessing, ritual, or ceremony that has the power to make holy what
God has declared to be unholy. All occult and false religious practices need to be renounced and rejected, and all objects associated
with them destroyed.

Some fear that to get rid of or destroy any such objects will
bring bad luck, misfortune, or a curse upon the one who destroys
them. They feel that either the person or spiritual being the object
represents, or even God Himself, will curse them and bring retri-

bution upon them if they destroy the charm, book, statue, or whatever. This is an understandable fear for those who have experienced firsthand the power that can be manifested through the occult and false religions. However be reassured that this is not the case at all.

If you have submitted yourself to God as outlined in these "Steps To Freedom," you are abiding under God's divine protection. You need not fear being harmed by any supernatural power as a result of your acting in obedience to God's command. As a matter of fact, it is by holding on to them and failing to renounce and destroy them that will bring about God's curse. In obedience to God's Word there is great blessing. In disobedience there is a curse (Deut 30:8-20). You may find it helpful to pray something like this:

Prayer:
"Heavenly Father, having rejected Satan and all occult and false religious doctrines and practices, and having received Your Son Jesus, as my Savior and Lord, I now confidently place myself under your divine protection and trust that You will keep me safe and that no spiritual threat or weapon brought against me will prosper. Thank you Lord that I am fully secure in Your hands. In Jesus name I pray. Amen."

God has set before us a choice. If Jesus is our Savior and Lord, then He must be obeyed. He is compassionate and understanding. He knows what we are thinking and feeling. He knows the inner struggle we experience and He is waiting to help us, if we will just call upon Him.

If you desire to do His will, if you really want to please Him, but you still find it hard to obey—the Lord understands. He knows your fears, doubts, and apprehension. He never promised you that following Him would be easy—but it is not impossible. Obedience is the only way forward into total freedom, and if you are willing, He will give you the strength and courage. He will stand beside you and watch over you. You won't be alone. And when you obey Him, you'll release Him to shower upon you all the blessings He longs to give you. Whatever the cost, it's worth it! So if you haven't taken this step yet, do so now.

Step Ten: Walk in Freedom
Deliverance from darkness and bondage into light and freedom is a wonderful gift to be cherished. Deliverance however, is also a walk and a way of life, not a once-for-all experience. If a person returns to the habitual practice of sin or to any of the forbidden practices and objects which they have renounced, they can lose that freedom and become subject again to demonic influence and bondage, which is often worse than before (Matt. 12: 43-45). The person who has been set free has a responsibility to continue to walk in fellowship and obedience with the Lord.

You may need to suggest some practical steps to help build up the life of the person in those areas in which they have been afflicted, and to protect the person from falling back into sins or situations whereby they could again come under the influence of evil spirits. Explaining how to walk in freedom as outlined below is extremely helpful. For many, arranging for follow-up counseling with a trained Christian professional is vital to walking in emotional wholeness and establishing new patterns of behavior that will ensure spiritual freedom. The following things are essential in maintaining a right relationship with the Lord and in maintaining spiritual freedom:

1) **Keep short accounts of sin.** We are not to sin, but if we do sin, we need to bring that sin immediately before the Lord in confession and repentance. Don't carry that sin around with you and save it up, but rather forsake it the moment you are aware of it. The Lord is faithful to forgive us and cleanse us of all unrighteousness. Even if you stumble, don't stay down, get right back up an keep on walking in the Lord (1 John 1:5-2:1).

2) **Read the Bible regularly.** Study to show yourself as an approved servant of the Lord. Through the Bible, God will reveal His will to you, warn you of dangers, and encourage your faith. Bring your life in line with its teachings (Acts 17:11; 2 Tim 3:15-16; John 14:21).

3) **Maintain open communication with God.** Pray regularly. Prayer is the best way to deepen your relationship with the Lord and to enjoy His fellowship. Talk to Him honestly from your heart, but always allow some quiet time to listen to His voice (John 15:7; 1 Cor 14:14-15; 1 Thes 5:17).

4) **Be filled with the Holy Spirit.** Yield to Him. The Spirit-filled life is marked by a repentant heart, an obedient spirit, a life of spiritual fruitfulness, and God's dynamic power. Ask Him to guide you and to empower you with gifts for effective service (Acts 1:8; Gal 5:16-17; Eph. 5:18; 1 Cor 12:7-11).

5) **Put on the full armor of God.** Clothe yourself with Him every day so that you'll be prepared to withstand

and resist all Satan's schemes (Eph. 6:10-18; Luke 10:19-20; 2 Cor 10:3-5; Jas 4:7).

6) **Spend time in spiritual fellowship** with other believers in the Body of Christ. Don't try to stand alone. Avoid spending time with those who are likely to entice you back to the things from which God has delivered you (Heb 10:25; Prov 13:20).

7) **Become part of a Christian church or fellowship** where Jesus Christ alone is worshiped and honored as Savior and Lord and the Bible is faithfully taught and followed. If you have been part of a religious group or organization that accepts or practices those things which are not sound biblical doctrine, come out from it (1 Tim 6:3-6; Col 2:8; Mk. 7:5-9, 13).

House Cleansing and Blessing

There is one additional matter which it is appropriate to address regarding freedom from occult and demonic bondage—a house cleansing and blessing.[6] In speaking of "house cleansing," I'm not referring to getting out the broom and dust rags, but rather to the cleansing of a house from the activity and influence of evil spirits.

We saw earlier, in examining the activity of evil spirits, that it is possible for demons to inhabit or dwell in certain places (Dan. 10:13; Rev. 2:13; 18:2). These demons may be responsible for a variety of spiritistic phenomena, such as apparitions or "ghosts,"[7]

---

[6] For a thorough discussion regarding protecting your home and family from spiritual pollution see the book by Eddie and Alice Smith, *Spiritual House Cleaning* (Ventura, CA: Regal Books, 2003).

[7] In discussing the phenomenon of "ghosts," Lester Sumrall has stated, "spirits of dead people do not become 'ghosts,' inhabiting houses, buildings, or graveyards. Any spirits that masquerade as ghosts, then, are demonic spirits." Sumrall, *Supernatural Principalities and Powers*, p. 110. This I feel, is the most accurate explanation.

and those manifestations typically associated with "hauntings."
Although "hauntings" are dismissed by many as pure superstition
or due to a wild imagination, as most of them actually are, nevertheless, there may well be genuine instances of demonic manifestations associated with particular places.[8] Such activity can be
frightening and very unsettling for those who live in the vicinity of
such things.

Also, demons may attempt to exercise a particular evil influence over those who are in or around what they consider their dwelling. It seems that these demonic manifestations are often (though
not always) associated with some past or present practice of occultism, occult-related paraphernalia, or false religious practices
and idols.

In response to this, Christian families who have recently been
freed from occult bondage, or those who move to a new location,
may find it prudent to set aside a special occasion for dedicating
their residence to the Lord—asking Him to sweep it clear of any
residual presence of the demonic and filling it with His own presence and peace.

Before doing this, all occult or non-Christian religious paraphernalia should be removed and destroyed as described in Step
Nine. This is an important part of the "cleansing" of the house
from those objects which may give evil spirits a reason or right to
stay.

---

[8] Dr. Cornelio Castillo states that demons may manifest their presence in
a place in several ways: 1) by a localized foul odor, 2) by a strongly
oppressive atmosphere, 3) by people being struck by some invisible force,
4) by the sensation of being touched in some manner, 5) by the visible
movement of objects, perhaps by telekinesis, 6) by objects being relo-
cated (thought to be lost or misplaced) from one room to another, 7) by
unexplainable sounds coming from a certain part of the house. From
class notes "Symptoms of Demonization" in the course Christian Response to Occultism, Asian Theological Seminary, Manila, 1991.

The occasion of dedication and blessing need not be anything elaborate; at the same time, it might provide an opportunity for fellowship with other believers and a witness to friends and neighbors. An example of such an informal house blessing, which we have used in our ministry on many occasions follows below. It is not necessary to follow any precise formula, this is only a model of what you might do.

The Blessing of a Residence

Songs of Joy and Praise

Opening Remarks (spoken by the host or member of the family explaining the purpose of the gathering)

Opening Prayer

Scripture Readings (possible selections: Deut 6:1-9; Ps 128; 122:6-9; Matt. 7:24-25)

Message from the Bible (optional)

Prayers of Thanksgiving (short prayers of thanksgiving offered by members of the family)

Prayer for Cleansing [9] (only after all occult, magical, and false religious objects have been removed from the house and destroyed. Bind and cast out the presence or influence of any evil spirits; forbid their reentry to the property to harm or harass the occupants. Ask the Lord to set a hedge of protection and security around the premises.)

Prayer:
"Heavenly Father, I acknowledge that You are the Lord of heaven and earth. In Your sovereign power

---

[9] Taken from: *The Bondage Breaker*, © 2000 by Neil T. Anderson, published by Harvest House Publishers, Eugene, OR. Used by permission.

and love, You have given me all things to enjoy. Thank you for this place to live. I claim my home as a place of spiritual safety for me and my family, and ask for Your protection from all attacks of the enemy. As a child of God, raised up and seated with Christ in the heavenly places, I command every evil spirit claiming ground in this place, based on the activities of past or present occupants, including me, to leave and never return. I renounce all curses and spells directed against this place. I ask You, heavenly Father, to post You warring angels around this place to guard it from any and all attempts to enter and disturb Your purposes for me and my family. I thank You, Lord, for doing this in the name of the Lord Jesus Christ. Amen."

Prayers of Blessing (you may go throughout the various rooms of the house asking blessings of the Lord appropriate to the function of each room, concluding with a final prayer of blessing. Or you may simply ask a prayer of blessing.)

Song(s) of Thanksgiving

Prayer of Dedication (commit the residence and those who live their to the glory of the Lord)

Benediction

Epilogue

As we have discovered in the course of this book, Satan and his demonic minions are a real enemy who fervently hate us. They will go to extreme lengths to trick us, to confuse us, to deceive us, and to entrap us. Among the foremost and most potent weapons in this satanic arsenal are the false religious beliefs and practices of the occult. The various expressions of magic, divination, and spiritism are not child's play, they are not "make-believe." They are not a joke, they are deadly serious. And although they may promise power, knowledge, pleasure, or peace, the promise is an empty one leading not to life, but to bondage, enslavement, and death.

If that were the whole story, it would be a tragic one indeed. Yet the truth is, there is a way out. There is a way to be set free from the bondage, to be released from the occult trap. That way is Jesus Christ! From the beginning, God saw the dilemma of humanity enslaved under the dominion of the Evil One and provided a way of freedom. He sent His one and only Son, Jesus, to redeem us and deliver us from the dominion of darkness. Jesus came to destroy all the works of the devil and His victory has been won! Christ's victory is yours and it is mine. It is for all who will put their trust entirely in Him.

This book has exposed the enemy to you. It has made you aware of how he operates. It has outlined for you the works of darkness known as the occult and evaluated them in the light of God's Word. Hopefully, it has taught you and provided you with sound biblical criteria for discerning those things which are of God and those things which draw their source of power and inspiration from Satan. And above all, it has set forth a way to experience spiritual freedom…steps that you can follow to break off the chains that bind you or which you can use to lead others to freedom.

I want to encourage you with hope. Jesus did not come to condemn, but to save and deliver. He loves you passionately and burns with a fervent desire for you to know the fullness of life and liberty in Him, to become…free at last!

Appendix A

Evaluation for Possible Signs and Symptoms of Demonization

*I*n the ministry of deliverance, one question that often arises is, "how do you know if it is really demonic?" Another similar question acknowledging the reality of psychological and emotional illness, is, "how do you tell the difference between what is a psychological disturbance and what is genuinely demonic?" To be honest, discerning the difference is not always easy and comes primarily by experience. Let's be straightforward about this—if the problem is an emotional or psychological one, you can try casting out demons all day and the person will never get any relief, because what they need is prayer and counseling. On the other hand, all the best counsel in the world will be of no avail, if the root cause of a person's problem is demonic bondage or control. What they need is the ministry of deliverance. So give time to the pre-ministry interview.

When conducting the pre-ministry interview, the following categorization of Demonic Symptoms which has been adapted from

Dr. Cornelio Castillo[1] may be a significant help. Dr. Castillo categorizes the symptoms into Primary and Secondary Symptoms. Primary Symptoms are purely demonic or supernatural symptoms and cannot be manifested by a psychological or psychiatric case. Secondary Symptoms are symptoms that may indicate demonic activity, but may also be seen in the mentally disturbed or purely psychological cases. The more accurate for determining demonization are, therefore, the primary symptoms. However it is not unusual to see a combination of both. The primary symptoms may seem exceptionally fantastic, but they have all been reported to have been witnessed by those involved in the ministry of deliverance.

Primary Symptoms

Unusual knowledge—the person may know some of our thoughts (mind-reading) or events that are happening far away; perhaps knowledge of past or future events. The demons encountered by Jesus knew who He was before He was introduced, the same was true of the apostle Paul in the book of Acts.

Unusual language ability—some have been known to speak Greek, Hebrew, Latin, and other languages when their only known language-dialects are their native language (a counterfeit to the genuine spiritual gift of tongues).

Unusual strength—some have demonstrated strength equivalent to that of several able-bodied men. We are talking here of a sustained show of strength rather than the adrenaline-caused, short-lived burst of strength.

---

[1] I am deeply indebted to Dr. Castillo for his insights which come from class lectures in the course "A Christian Response to Occultism," Dr. Cornelio Castillo, Asian Theological Seminary, Quezon City, Philippines, 1991.

Hypnotizing eyes—some have been know to have been virtually immobilized by just looking at the eyes of a demonized person. This is different from glazed eyes or a blank vacant stare which can also be seen in a purely psychological case.

Sudden change of body weight—some may become unusually heavy or unusually light for their body size; this change may occur in a span of a few minutes to a few hours.

Change of voice or multiple voices—females may speak like males or adults may speak like young children with no strained artificiality to it. Some kind of a forced change may be observed among the insane, however, a natural, effortless change of voice accompanied by what usually sounds like wise pronouncements or sarcastic statements are signs of the presence of a spirit in a person. Sometimes it may sound as if several voices are speaking all at the same time.

Ability to float or levitate—the act of rising from the floor usually begins with the person arching his/her back until only both ends of the body touch the floor. When levitating is done by someone sitting down or standing up, the act is participated in willingly by the person. If the person is lying down on the floor and begins to be lifted up, they are not a participant in the act.

Animal sounds—some will bark or howl like a dog, croak like a frog, etc. There are times when the animal sounds are not coming from the mouth of the person but from another area inside or outside the house. This should not cause fear as this is usually a sign that the enemy has resorted to distractions and deception since he has already recognized his defeat.

Sudden appearance of marks on the body—in some cases of demonization, the person's body will show welts, or other marks that were not there before. Often, these conditions will worsen as you command the spirit to come out. These will disappear when the person is freed from demonic power.

Unseen force throwing the person—a person can of course roll over, bend, and do things like that, however, one just cannot lift and throw oneself to another place—some kind of a force is throwing them around. In cases such as this, it is usually true that the person may have gotten involved with the occult, or may have actually made a pact with a spirit and has received something as a token of that relationship. It can be a power object, such as a ring, a stone, a power-word, a phrase to recite in certain situations. Be sure to ask about these.

An apparently very intense internal conflict—this can be observed physically. Unlike a psychotic who loses contact with reality when something like this happens, the demonized person is aware of your presence and you can actually talk with them very sensibly except that they have no control over the battle raging within them.

Objects coming out of mouth or nose—when sorcery is involved, sometimes things such as human hair, sand, pebbles, insects, and other objects can come out of the mouth or nose. It is easy to dismiss this as a product of a fertile imagination, but that can't be said by those who have actually seen this.

Seemingly impossible contortion of the body or parts of the body (such as the head turned beyond its natural range of motion).

Bi-location—the person may be reported to appear in more than one place at the same time. In this case the indication is that the demon is not inside, but is only accompanying the person.

Teleporting—person disappears from one place and appears at another as if by magic. The demon is usually not inside, but outside the body.

Eyes become all white

Telekinetic/Psychokinetic movements—moving objects by apparent mental power. The power is not actually mind-power, but demonic power, either assisting the person from the outside, or empowering them from within.

Missile-like spittle or vomit

Unearthly, vile, bad odor

Counterfeit spiritual gifts—apparent spiritual gifts, but makes use of occult means or has contradictory lifestyle/behavior.

Secondary Symptoms

♦ Dislike of anything associated with religion/Christianity

♦ Foul, vulgar language (especially when this is out of character for the person)

♦ Unhygienic practices and appearance

♦ Sexual display or invitation

♦ Excessively argumentative (especially when this is a new behavior)

♦ Conversation with unseen beings

♦ Violence (especially when this is out of character for the person)

♦ Glazed eyes, vacant stare

♦ Persistent, often violent, unjustified jealousy

♦ Unusual behavior (i.e., animal like movements; constant motion; unable to sit still; pacing; unusual postures or gestures)

Most of the usual insanity indicators may be classified under the Secondary Symptoms.

Other Possible Indicators

The person may indicate that they:

♦ Feels something within them controlling their actions or speech

♦ Feels someone is reading their thoughts

♦ Cannot pray or that they have been cut off from God
♦ Cannot read the Bible, or understand it anymore; that their mind
  becomes blank when they try, or they get headaches or become
  unusually sleepy

Complete the pre-ministry interview using the following Evaluation Checklist as a guide. But remember that some demonization
cases may not show any symptoms until the ministry session begins.

Evaluation Checklist
for Suspected Demonic Affliction

Name:_____ Age:_____
Sex:_____Marital Status:_____
Religious Affiliation:_____

Preliminary Interview

1. Why is there a suspicion that the person is demonized?

2. Has the person ever been involved with:
    a. spiritism   Yes   No
    If yes, specify:_____

    b. magic   Yes   No
    If yes, specify:_____

    c. divination   Yes   No
    If yes, specify:_____

d. cults, paganism, false religions   Yes   No
If yes, specify:_____

3. Have any members of the person's family (including parents, grandparents, great-grandparents) ever been involved with:

a. spiritism   Yes   No
If yes, specify:_____

b. magic   Yes   No
If yes, specify:_____

c. divination   Yes   No
If yes, specify:_____

d. cults, paganism, false religions   Yes   No
If yes, specify:_____

4. Has the person experienced or been involved with any of the following:

Sin (of a serious, persistent,
compulsive, or habitual nature)   Yes   No

unrighteous anger, rage, violence   Yes   No

self-hatred and hatred of others   Yes   No

revenge, unforgiveness   Yes   No

sexual immorality, lust,
pornography   Yes   No

perversions (e.g., transvestism,
homosexuality, bestiality)   Yes   No

drug or alcohol abuse   Yes   No

other:_____

Victim of Other Person's Sin
incest   Yes   No

rape   Yes   No

homosexual rape   Yes   No

severe or frightening physical
violence, physical abuse   Yes   No

other:_____

Curses
Serious, persistent verbal abuse
(by friends, relatives, etc.)   Yes   No

called curses upon self   Yes   No

curses by magic   Yes   No

other:_____

Trauma

abandonment or rejection by parents	Yes	No
serious accident	Yes	No
extremely frightening or terrorizing experience	Yes	No

other:_____

Direct Demonic Attack

telekinetic or psychokinetic movement of objects	Yes	No
apparitions	Yes	No
disembodied voices	Yes	No
sensations of physical contact with a spirit being	Yes	No

other:_____

Comments:

Primary Symptoms

(purely demonic and spiritual in nature and cannot be manifested by a psychological or psychiatric case)

Degree or Intensity of Symptom:
   1=mild, normal, average   5=severe, extraordinary, serious

1. Unusual knowledge   1 2 3 4 5

2. Unusual language ability   1 2 3 4 5

3. Unusual strength   1 2 3 4 5

4. Hypnotizing eyes   1 2 3 4 5

5. Sudden change of body
    weight (in hours)   1 2 3 4 5

6. Change of voice or multiple voices   1 2 3 4 5

7. Ability to float or levitate   1 2 3 4 5

8. Unusual length of exposed tongue   1 2 3 4 5

9. Animal sounds   1 2 3 4 5

10. Sudden appearance of marks   1 2 3 4 5
    welts, bruises

11. Unseen force throwing
    the person   1 2 3 4 5

12. An apparently very intense
    internal conflict   1   2   3   4   5

13. Objects coming out of
    mouth or nose   1   2   3   4   5

14. Seemingly impossible contortion
    of the body, head turned beyond
    natural range   1   2   3   4   5

15. Bi-location—the person appears in
    several places at the same time   1   2   3   4   5

16. Teleporting—person disappears
    from one place and appears at
    another as if by magic   1   2   3   4   5

17. Eyes become all white   1   2   3   4   5

18. Telekinetic/Psychokinetic
    movements—moving objects
    by apparent mental power   1   2   3   4   5

19. Missile-like spittle or vomit   1   2   3   4   5

20. Unearthly, vile, bad odor   1   2   3   4   5

21. Counterfeit spiritual gifts apparent
    spiritual gifts, but makes use of
    occult means or has contradictory
    lifestyle/behavior   1   2   3   4   5

Secondary Symptoms

(may indicate demonic activity, but may also be seen in purely psychological cases or cases of mental/emotional disturbance)

Degree or Intensity of Symptom:
   1=mild, normal, average   5=severe, extraordinary, serious

1. Dislike of anything associated
    with religion/Christianity   1   2   3   4   5

2. Foul, vulgar language
    (especially when this is out of
    character for the person)   1   2   3   4   5

3. Unhygienic practices/appearance   1   2   3   4   5

4. Sexual display or invitation   1   2   3   4   5

5. Excessively argumentative
    (especially when this is
    a new behavior)   1   2   3   4   5

6. Conversation with unseen beings   1   2   3   4   5

7. Violence (especially when this is
    out of character for the person)   1   2   3   4   5

8. Glazed eyes, vacant stare   1   2   3   4   5

9. Persistent, often violent,
    unjustified jealousy   1   2   3   4   5

10. Unusual behavior (i.e., animal like
    movements; constant motion;
    unable to sit still; pacing;
    unusual postures or gestures)   1   2   3   4   5

Other Possible Indicators

(may indicate demonic activity, but may also be seen in purely psychological cases or cases of mental/emotional disturbance)

Degree or Intensity of Symptom:
  1=mild, normal, average   5=severe, extraordinary, serious

The person may indicate that they:
  1. Feel something within them
     controlling their actions or speech   1   2   3   4   5

  2. Feels someone is reading
     their thoughts   1   2   3   4   5

  3. Cannot pray or feeling
     cut off from God   1   2   3   4   5

  4. Cannot read or understand the
     Bible. Their mind becomes blank
     or they experience headaches or
     unusual sleepiness when trying to
     read Scripture.   1   2   3   4   5

Checklist for Involvement in the Occult

Instructions

Read through the following list carefully. Place a checkmark in the appropriate box and circle any of the practices in bold letters that you have specifically been involved with.

Divination

☐ had your fortune read by use of: **cards** (tarot), **tea leaves, crystal ball, palm reading, I Ching, Pyromancy, candle wax**, or any other means

☐ consulted a **geomancer** or used **feng shui**

☐ followed **astrology**, read your **horoscope**, used or followed signs of the **zodiac**

☐ practiced locating something by means of radiesthesia—**divining rod** (forked stick, etc.) or **pendulum**; (also known as dowsing)

☐ used a **crystal ball** or **magic mirror** in order to discover the unknown

❏ consulted a **seer, fortune teller, medium,** or **psychic**

❏ followed **omens, signs, numerology** or **auspicious days or dates** as a means of guidance or making decisions

Magic

❏ sought healing through **magic chants, magic potions, special water** or **magical herbs**

❏ sought healing through a **medium, psychic healer,** or anyone who practices **"spirit healing"**

❏ sought healing through "new age" techniques such as **acupuncture, iridology, pranic healing,** etc.

❏ practiced **white magic** or **black magic**

❏ practiced **love magic** or the casting of **spells** or **hexes,** either to help or to harm someone or sought the assistance of someone who did

❏ worn or carried any **charm, medallion, amulet, talisman** for protection or good luck

❏ kept in your home, business, or automobile any **charm** or **talisman (picture, figurine** or **statue)** to give safety, prosperity, good fortune, etc.

❏ received or used **magic letters,** chain letters, letters of protection, etc.

❏ participated in the rites or rituals of any form of **witchcraft** or **Satanism**

❑ made a **blood pact, blood oath,** or **blood subscription**

Spiritism

❑ experimented with or practiced **telepathy** or **mind reading**

❑ practiced **ESP, clairvoyance, sixth sense/second sight,** or **psychometry**

❑ had repeated accurate **premonitions** or **cognition** (special knowledge) of future events

❑ attended a **seance** or spiritualist meeting

❑ attempted to contact or communicate with anyone who has died or with spirits, practiced **necromancy,** conjuring the dead

❑ consulted the **Ouija board, "spirit of the glass,"** out of curiosity or in earnest

❑ consulted a **medium** or anyone who uses a **trance, hypnosis,** or **pendulum** for diagnosis or treatment

❑ sought to locate a missing object or person by consulting someone who has psychic powers or by consulting the dead

❑ practiced **telekinesis** or **levitation**

❑ practiced **soul travel** or **astral projection**

❑ practiced mental suggestion or remote influence on the mind of others

❑ entered into a **trance,** spoken in a trance, or practiced **automatic writing**

❑ sought help from a "**spirit guide**" or practiced "**channeling**"

❑ experienced or witnessed **apports**, **materializations**, or **apparitions**, **ghosts**, **poltergeists**, or other spirit beings such as dwarves, ogres, fairies, etc.

❑ by prayer, invitation, or consecration asked anyone living or dead (other than Jesus Christ) into your life to control or guide you, or have been consecrated to another spirit being, "god," or "saint"

❑ used **crystals** as a means of obtaining well-being

Other Occult-Related
❑ experimented with or practiced **hypnosis** upon yourself or others, or have been hypnotized

❑ taken any kind of **mind-altering drug**

❑ practiced **yoga** or explored the religious or psychic side of **martial arts**

❑ played occult games such as **Dungeons and Dragons**, etc., including fantasy role-playing games (including video versions)

❑ possess or wear jewelry or clothing with occult-related symbols or slogans

❑ made pilgrimages to shrines, temples, or other "holy" places such as mountains, caves, sacred springs, etc.

❑ practiced use of "pyramid power"

❑ read or possessed occult or spiritualist literature on: magic, witchcraft, cabala, voodoo, astrology, dream interpretation, reincarnation, fortune-telling, numerology, metaphysics, cosmic consciousness, ESP, Psychic phenomena, New Age, Silva Mind Control, EST, or books such as: The Gnostic Gospels, The Aquarian Gospel of Jesus Christ, etc.

❑ known anyone in your family (i.e., parents, grandparents, great-grandparents) who are/were involved in the occult or reputed to have any special powers

❑ practiced **Maharishi Technology (TM)**, use of **mantra**, or any other kind of **passive meditation**, or tried to combine **Eastern meditation techniques** with Christianity (e.g., visualization, etc.)

❑ put your **mind in** a **passive state** (blanking your mind) in order to pray or seek guidance

❑ had a **reincarnation** or "**life**" **reading**

Cults and Non-Christian Religions
(incompatible with historic, orthodox Christianity)

❑ **possessed any object used in animistic or pagan** (non-Christian) **religious rituals** (religious curios); or **images**, **pictures**, or **statues representing deities or persons** that are considered to have special powers (even if they are simply considered "art" or "decorations"), e.g., Buddhas, etc.

❑ **revered, venerated, worshiped, brought offerings, or prayed to a picture, statue, or any other graven image**

Have you ever attended meetings, participated in rites, or read the magazines or literature of any of the following cults:

❏ **Mormon** (Latter Day Saints)—Book of Mormon, Doctrines and Covenants, Pearl of Great Price

❏ **Jehovah's Witness**—"Watch Tower", "Awake"

❏ **Rosicrucians**

❏ **Unity**

❏ **Christian Science**—writings of Mary Baker Eddy

❏ **Church Universal and Triumphant**—writings of Elizabeth Clair Prophet

❏ **Children of God**—writings of David Moses

❏ **Theosophy** (metaphysics)—"Theosophical Digest"

❏ **Worldwide Church of God** (Armstongism)—"Plain Truth"

❏ **Unification Church** (Moonies)

❏ **Scientology**—writings of L. Ron Hubbard

❏ **SOMM** (Science of Mind and Man)

❏ **Freemasonry** (York Rite, Scottish Rite, associated organizations—Shrine, Eastern Star, Demolay, Rainbow Girls)

❏ other **Lodges, Secret Societies, Fraternities, Sororities**, or **Gangs**

❏ **The Way International**

Have you ever been a member of or participated in any non-Christian religion:

❏ **Islam**

❏ **Hinduism**

❏ **Buddhism**

❏ **Taoism**

❏ **Shintoism**

❑ **Confucianism**
❑ **Sikhism**

Have you ever believed or participated in any of the following "secular religions":
❑ **Atheism**
❑ **Agnosticism**
❑ **Skepticism**
❑ **Marxism**
❑ **Secular Humanism**
❑ **Existentialism**

Subject Index

witchcraft, 81, 121-122
Word of God, 142-143, 158, 173
word of knowledge, 138
word of wisdom, 138
work of knowledge, 172
World War II, 32

Y
Yin and Yang, 85, 119
Yocum, Bruce, 163
yoga, 74, 84, 86, 87

Z
zodiac, 91, 97